# Tail-Wagging Treats: A DIY Dog Food Feast

## Simple Recipes for a Healthy and Happy Pup

# Emily Reynolds

© Copyright 2024 - All rights reserved.

The content contained within this book may not be reproduced, duplicated or transmitted without direct written permission from the author or the publisher.

Under no circumstances will any blame or legal responsibility be held against the publisher, or author, for any damages, reparation, or monetary loss due to the information contained within this book, either directly or indirectly.

**Legal Notice:**

This book is copyright protected. It is only for personal use. You cannot amend, distribute, sell, use, quote or paraphrase any part, or the content within this book, without the consent of the author or publisher.

**Disclaimer Notice:**

Please note the information contained within this document is for educational and entertainment purposes only. All effort has been executed to present accurate, up to date, reliable, complete information. No warranties of any kind are declared or implied. Readers acknowledge that the author is not engaging in the rendering of legal, financial, medical or professional advice. The content within this book has been derived from various sources. Please consult a licensed professional before attempting any techniques outlined in this book.

By reading this document, the reader agrees that under no circumstances is the author responsible for any losses, direct or indirect, that are incurred as a result of the use of information contained within this document, including, but not limited to, errors, omissions, or inaccuracies.

# Table of Contents

# INTRODUCTION

Welcome to "Tail-Wagging Treats: A DIY Dog Food Feast – Simple Recipes for a Healthy and Happy Pup," your guide to unlocking the world of canine culinary delights. In this e-book, we embark on a journey to revolutionize the way you care for your furry companion by exploring the art of crafting wholesome and delicious homemade meals tailored to meet your dog's nutritional needs.

Our canine friends deserve the very best, and what better way to show them love than by preparing nutritious, mouthwatering treats right in your own kitchen? With a focus on simplicity and health, this e-book offers a collection of easy-to-follow recipes designed to keep your pup not only satisfied but also thriving.

In the opening chapters, we delve into the fundamentals of understanding your dog's nutritional requirements, exploring essential ingredients that contribute to their well-being, and introducing the basic tools and equipment needed for successful homemade dog food preparation. Whether you're a seasoned chef or a kitchen novice, we provide valuable insights into tailoring diets for different breeds, ensuring that your pup receives the optimal nutrients for a vibrant and happy life.

The heart of this e-book lies in its carefully curated chapters, each dedicated to specific meals and treats tailored to different times of the day and occasions. From protein-packed breakfast bowls to gourmet dinner delights, every recipe is crafted with love and attention to detail. We also cater to special occasions with birthday cake bonanzas and holiday feasts, because our dogs deserve to celebrate with us.

Throughout this journey, we address common concerns such as dietary restrictions and provide guidance on transitioning your pup to a homemade diet. With safety guidelines, nutritional insights, and expert tips, "Tail-Wagging Treats" empowers you to become your dog's personal chef, fostering a stronger bond and a healthier, happier life for your beloved four-legged friend. Get ready to unleash your culinary creativity and embark on a delightful adventure in the kitchen for the well-being of your tail-wagging companion.

# CHAPTER I

# Understanding Your Dog's Nutritional Needs

## Overview of Dog Nutrition

Nutrition plays a crucial role in the overall health and well-being of dogs. As beloved companions and members of the family, dogs rely on their owners to provide them with a balanced and nutritious diet to support their physical and mental health. Understanding the key components of dog nutrition is essential for responsible pet ownership and ensuring the longevity of our canine friends.

Protein is a fundamental building block in a dog's diet, essential for the growth, repair, and maintenance of tissues. High-quality protein sources, such as meat, poultry, and fish, provide the amino acids necessary for these vital processes. While the exact protein requirements vary based on factors such as age, breed, and activity level, it is generally agreed that a significant portion of a dog's diet should consist of protein-rich foods.

Fats are another crucial component of a dog's diet, serving as a concentrated source of energy. Healthy fats, such as those found in fish oil and flaxseed, contribute to a shiny coat, support brain function, and aid in the absorption of fat-soluble vitamins. Maintaining an appropriate balance of fats in a dog's diet is important, as excessive fat intake can lead to obesity and related health issues.

Carbohydrates, while not as essential as protein and fats, play a role in providing dogs with energy. Common sources of carbohydrates in dog food include grains, vegetables, and legumes. However, it's essential to select high-quality carbohydrates that are easily digestible, as some dogs may have sensitivities or allergies to certain grains. Additionally, monitoring the overall carbohydrate content is crucial, as excessive carbohydrates can contribute to obesity and other health issues.

Vitamins and minerals are micronutrients that play a vital role in various physiological processes, including immune function, bone health, and energy metabolism. Dog owners should ensure that their pet's diet contains an adequate supply of essential vitamins and minerals. This can be achieved through a balanced and varied diet, as different foods provide different micronutrients. However, it's important not to over-supplement, as excessive intake of certain vitamins and minerals can be harmful.

Water is perhaps the most critical nutrient for dogs. Proper hydration is essential for digestion, nutrient absorption, temperature regulation, and overall cellular function. Dog owners must provide their pets with access to clean and fresh water at all times. Monitoring water intake is particularly important in hot weather or for dogs with certain health conditions that may increase their water needs.

Special attention must be given to the unique nutritional requirements of different life stages and breeds. Puppies, for example, require a diet that supports their rapid growth and development, while senior dogs may benefit from foods designed to address age-related issues. Large breeds may have specific nutritional needs to support their bone health, and small breeds may require diets that cater to their smaller size and metabolism.

It's crucial for dog owners to be aware of their pet's individual needs and any specific health concerns that may influence dietary requirements. Regular veterinary check-ups can provide valuable insights into a dog's overall health and nutritional needs. In some cases, veterinarians may recommend specialized diets to address specific health conditions, such as allergies, digestive issues, or weight management.

In conclusion, maintaining optimal dog nutrition is a multifaceted task that requires careful consideration of various factors. A well-balanced diet, rich in high-quality proteins, fats, carbohydrates, vitamins, and minerals, is essential for promoting a dog's overall health and longevity. Owners must tailor their pet's diet to meet individual needs, taking into account factors such as age, breed, activity level, and any underlying health conditions. With proper nutrition, dogs can thrive, leading happy and healthy lives as cherished members of the family.

## Key Nutrients for a Healthy Dog

Ensuring the health and well-being of our canine companions involves providing them with a well-rounded and nutritionally balanced diet. Dogs, like humans, require a combination of essential nutrients to thrive. From proteins that build and repair tissues to vitamins that support various bodily functions, each nutrient plays a crucial role in maintaining a dog's overall health.

Protein is a cornerstone of a healthy dog's diet, serving as the primary building block for tissues, muscles, and organs. Dogs are omnivores, meaning they can derive protein from both animal and plant sources. High-quality animal proteins, such as those found in meat, fish, and poultry, provide the essential amino acids that dogs cannot produce on their own. Adequate protein intake is particularly important for growing puppies, highly active dogs, and those in recovery from illness or injury.

Fats are another vital component of a dog's diet, serving as a concentrated source of energy. Healthy fats, including omega-3 and omega-6 fatty acids, play a crucial role in maintaining a dog's skin and coat health. Sources of these beneficial fats include fish oil, flaxseed, and chicken fat. While fats are an essential part of a dog's diet, it's crucial to maintain a proper balance, as excessive fat intake can contribute to obesity and related health issues.

Carbohydrates provide dogs with a readily available source of energy. While dogs can survive without carbohydrates, they can be a valuable part of a well- balanced diet. Common carbohydrate sources in dog food include grains, vegetables, and legumes. However, it's important to choose easily digestible and high-quality carbohydrates to avoid potential sensitivities. Monitoring carbohydrate intake is crucial, as excessive amounts can contribute to weight gain.

Vitamins and minerals are micronutrients that play a crucial role in various physiological processes. For example, vitamin A is essential for vision, vitamin D aids in calcium absorption for strong bones, and vitamin C supports the immune system. Minerals such as calcium, phosphorus, and potassium are vital for bone health, nerve function, and fluid balance. A varied and balanced diet that includes a range of foods can help ensure dogs receive an adequate supply of these essential micronutrients.

Water is often overlooked but is perhaps the most critical nutrient for dogs. Proper hydration is essential for digestion, nutrient absorption, temperature regulation, and overall cellular function. Dog owners must provide their pets with access to clean and fresh water at all times. Monitoring water intake is particularly important during hot weather or for dogs with certain health conditions that may increase their water needs.

Tailoring a dog's diet to their life stage is crucial for meeting specific nutritional requirements. Puppies, with their rapid growth and development, require a diet higher in protein and calories than adult dogs. Senior dogs may benefit from diets that address age-related issues, such as joint health and cognitive function. Large and small breeds may have unique nutritional needs based on their size and metabolism. Understanding these life stage and breed-specific requirements is key to providing optimal nutrition for dogs.

Regular veterinary check-ups are essential for monitoring a dog's health and addressing any specific dietary needs. Veterinarians can provide guidance on selecting the right food for a dog's individual requirements and may recommend specialized diets to manage conditions such as allergies, digestive issues, or weight concerns. Nutritional counseling from a veterinary professional can be invaluable for ensuring a dog's diet aligns with their overall health goals.

In conclusion, key nutrients are essential for maintaining the health and vitality of our canine companions. A well-balanced diet that includes adequate protein, fats, carbohydrates, vitamins, minerals, and water is fundamental to supporting a dog's overall well-being. Understanding the specific needs of individual dogs, based on factors like age, breed, and health status, allows pet owners to make informed choices about their furry friends' nutrition. By prioritizing proper nutrition, dog owners can contribute to the longevity and happiness of their beloved pets, fostering a strong and lasting bond between humans and dogs.

## Tailoring Diets for Different Dog Breeds and Sizes

Dogs, with their diverse breeds and sizes, exhibit a wide range of nutritional needs. Recognizing and addressing these specific dietary requirements is essential for ensuring the health and well-being of our four-legged companions. The nutritional demands of a small breed, such as a Chihuahua, vastly differ from those of a large breed like a Great Dane. Tailoring diets to accommodate the unique characteristics of various dog breeds and sizes is a critical aspect of responsible pet ownership.

Small breeds, often characterized by their petite stature and energetic disposition, necessitate diets that cater to their higher metabolic rates and smaller stomach capacities. These dogs often burn more calories per pound than larger breeds, requiring food that is nutrient-dense to meet their energy needs. Protein content is particularly important for small breeds, as it supports their muscle development and overall vitality. Owners of small dogs should opt for high-quality, small-sized kibble that is easily manageable for their tiny jaws. Additionally, small breeds may be prone to dental issues, making dental health considerations an essential factor when selecting appropriate dog food.

On the other end of the spectrum, large and giant breeds present their own set of nutritional challenges. These dogs, such as Saint Bernards or Great Danes, experience slower growth rates but have a longer growth period compared to smaller breeds. Therefore, their diets must strike a delicate balance between providing enough nutrients for proper development and avoiding excessive intake that could lead to orthopedic issues. Controlled levels of calcium and phosphorus are crucial for large breeds to support healthy bone growth and prevent skeletal abnormalities. Additionally, large breeds are more susceptible to joint issues, making diets with added glucosamine and chondroitin beneficial for maintaining joint health.

Medium-sized breeds, falling between the extremes of small and large, have nutritional needs that align with their moderate size and activity levels. A balanced diet that includes an appropriate mix of protein, fats, and carbohydrates is generally suitable for medium-sized dogs. Tailoring the diet to the individual dog's activity level, age, and health status remains essential, as variations within the medium-sized category can still impact nutritional requirements.

Puppies, regardless of their eventual size, have distinct nutritional needs during their growth and development stages. Small breed puppies mature more quickly than larger breeds, reaching adulthood sooner. This accelerated growth requires a puppy food with higher levels of protein, fat, and calories to support their rapid development. In contrast, large breed puppies require controlled nutrient levels to prevent excessive growth rates that could contribute to orthopedic issues. Specialized puppy formulas designed for specific breed sizes help address these variations and provide the necessary nutrients for a healthy start in life.

Senior dogs, irrespective of size, often experience changes in metabolism, dental health, and joint function. Adjusting their diets to accommodate these changes is crucial for maintaining their overall well-being. Senior dog foods typically have reduced calorie content to prevent weight gain, and they may include joint supplements to support mobility. Dental health becomes a focus as well, with kibble shapes and sizes designed to promote chewing and reduce plaque buildup.

Beyond size, certain breeds may be predisposed to specific health issues, influencing their dietary requirements. For example, breeds prone to food allergies or sensitivities may benefit from hypoallergenic diets that avoid common allergens. Breeds with a tendency for obesity may require weight management formulas that control calorie intake while providing essential nutrients. Understanding the breed-specific predispositions allows dog owners to proactively address potential health concerns through appropriate nutrition.

In recent years, there has been a growing trend towards breed-specific dog foods. These formulations claim to cater specifically to the nutritional needs of certain breeds based on their unique characteristics and potential health risks. While the concept is intriguing, it's essential for pet owners to approach such products with a discerning eye. Individual variations within a breed, as well as the dog's specific age, activity level, and health condition, may still necessitate customization of the diet beyond what a generic breed-specific formula can offer.

Ultimately, tailoring diets for different dog breeds and sizes requires a nuanced approach that considers the individual dog's characteristics. Consulting with veterinarians to determine the specific needs of a dog based on factors such as age, size, breed, and health status is crucial.

Regular veterinary check-ups can provide valuable insights into a dog's overall health and nutritional requirements, allowing for adjustments to the diet as needed.

In conclusion, recognizing and addressing the diverse nutritional needs of different dog breeds and sizes is paramount for responsible pet ownership. Small breeds, large breeds, and those in between each require specific attention to ensure their diets support their unique characteristics and promote optimal health. From controlling nutrient levels for growth to managing weight and addressing breed-specific health concerns, tailoring diets plays a pivotal role in the longevity and well-being of our canine companions. As our understanding of canine nutrition continues to evolve, so too does our ability to provide personalized and targeted diets that contribute to the health and happiness of dogs of all shapes and sizes.

# CHAPTER II

# Essential Ingredients for DIY Dog Food

## High-Quality Proteins

Proteins often called the building blocks of life, play a fundamental role in the health and well-being of all living organisms, including our canine companions. In dog nutrition, the importance of high-quality proteins cannot be overstated. Dogs, as omnivores, rely on a combination of animal and plant-based proteins to meet their dietary requirements. The term "high-quality proteins" denotes those protein sources that provide essential amino acids in optimal proportions, supporting the various physiological processes crucial for a dog's overall health.

The significance of proteins lies in their composition of amino acids, the basic structural units necessary for tissue growth, repair, and maintenance. Essential amino acids are those that dogs cannot synthesize within their bodies and must obtain through their diet. Animal proteins, such as those derived from meat, fish, and poultry, are considered complete proteins as they contain all the essential amino acids in the required proportions. These proteins support a dog's muscle development, immune function, and overall vitality.

The digestibility of proteins is another critical factor in assessing their quality. High-quality proteins are rich in essential amino acids and easily digestible, allowing for efficient absorption and utilization by the dog's body. Protein digestibility is influenced by factors such as source, processing methods, and the overall composition of the diet. Since dogs have varying degrees of tolerance to different protein sources, dog owners must select protein-rich foods well-tolerated by their pets.

While animal proteins are a primary source of high-quality proteins for dogs, plant-based proteins also contribute to their overall protein intake. Grains, legumes, and vegetables contain proteins that, when combined, can complement each other to provide a well-balanced amino acid profile. However, it's crucial to ensure that the plant-based proteins are easily digestible and bioavailable to meet a dog's nutritional needs. Additionally, some dogs may have sensitivities or allergies to specific plant proteins, necessitating careful selection based on individual tolerances.

The protein requirements for dogs vary based on age, breed, activity level, and overall health. With their rapid growth and development, Puppies require higher protein intake to support the building of tissues and organs. Highly active dogs, such as those involved in agility or working roles, also have increased protein needs to keep their energy requirements and muscle maintenance. Conversely, senior dogs may benefit from slightly reduced protein levels, particularly if they have kidney issues, as lower protein intake can help manage renal function.

The debate surrounding animal-based versus plant-based dog diets has gained attention recently. While some argue for the benefits of plant-based diets from an environmental and ethical standpoint, others emphasize the nutritional completeness of animal-based proteins. It is essential to approach the topic nuancedly, recognizing that dogs are adaptable and can thrive on various diet compositions. However, when opting for plant-based proteins, careful formulation and supplementation may be required to ensure that all essential amino acids are adequately provided.

Protein quality is closely tied to dog food's sourcing and processing ingredients. High-quality dog foods prioritize using premium protein sources, often listing specific meats or meat meals as the primary ingredients. Meat meals, produced by rendering and drying meat, can be concentrated protein sources, providing essential amino acids in a condensed form. On the other hand, lower-quality dog foods may contain unspecified or generic meat by-products, which may need more nutritional completeness and digestibility than premium protein sources.

The popularity of raw and fresh dog food diets has further emphasized the importance of high-quality proteins. Proponents of these diets argue that raw or minimally processed meats better retain the natural nutrients and enzymes beneficial for a dog's health. However, it's crucial to approach raw diets cautiously, considering the risk of bacterial contamination and the potential for nutritional imbalances. Consulting with veterinarians to ensure the formulation of a balanced and nutritionally complete diet is particularly important for raw or homemade dog food.

Specialized diets catering to specific health conditions or life stages may also adjust protein levels and sources. For example, dogs with food allergies or sensitivities may benefit from limited-ingredient diets that use novel protein sources to minimize the risk of adverse reactions. Prescription diets for dogs with kidney disease may have controlled protein levels to manage the strain on the kidneys. Understanding the specific nutritional needs of individual dogs and consulting with veterinarians can guide dog owners in selecting the most appropriate diet for their pets.

In conclusion, high-quality proteins form the bedrock of a nutritious and well-balanced dog diet. The essential amino acids provided by these proteins are crucial for supporting various physiological functions, including muscle development, immune function, and overall vitality. Whether sourced from animal or plant-based ingredients, the key is to ensure that proteins are easily digestible and meet the individual dietary requirements of dogs based on factors such as age, breed, and health status. With a focus on protein quality, dog owners can contribute to their beloved canine companions' overall health and longevity.

## Beneficial Carbohydrates

Carbohydrates, often regarded as the body's primary energy source, play a crucial role in dogs' overall health and well-being. While the spotlight in canine nutrition often falls on proteins and fats, incorporating beneficial carbohydrates into a dog's diet should be considered. Carbohydrates encompass diverse nutrients, including grains, vegetables, and legumes, each contributing unique benefits to a dog's overall nutritional profile.

One of the primary functions of carbohydrates in a dog's diet is to provide energy. Dogs are known for their boundless energy, and carbohydrates are a readily available and efficient fuel source for their active lifestyles. Grains such as rice, oats, and barley, and vegetables like sweet potatoes and peas are familiar sources of complex carbohydrates that release energy slowly, providing a sustained fuel source for dogs engaged in various activities.

While dogs are classified as omnivores, meaning they can derive nutrients from animal and plant sources, the specific carbohydrate requirements can vary based on age, breed, and activity level. With their higher energy needs and rapid growth, Puppies may benefit from a diet with slightly higher carbohydrate content to support their developmental stages. Conversely, less active senior dogs might require diets with a lower carbohydrate content to prevent excess calorie intake.

Fiber, a carbohydrate in plant-based foods, is another critical component of a dog's diet. Beneficial for digestive health, fiber aids in regulating bowel movements, preventing constipation, and promoting overall gastrointestinal function. Familiar sources of fiber in dog food include vegetables, fruits, and whole grains. Dietary fiber is particularly beneficial for dogs with sensitive stomachs or those prone to gastrointestinal issues.

Choosing high-quality, easily digestible carbohydrates is critical to ensuring that dogs derive maximum nutritional benefit from their diet. While grains have been a traditional source of carbohydrates in dog food, there has been a growing trend toward grain-free and novel carbohydrate sources, such as sweet potatoes and legumes. Dog owners need to consider their pets' individual dietary needs and sensitivities when selecting carbohydrates, as some dogs may thrive on traditional grains. In contrast, others may benefit from alternative sources.

Carbohydrates also contribute to the palatability and texture of dog food. Including carbohydrates in kibble formulations helps create a well-balanced and appealing texture for dogs, encouraging them to consume their meals enthusiastically. This palatability factor becomes particularly important when dealing with picky eaters or dogs with specific taste preferences. Dog food manufacturers often formulate their products with a combination of proteins, fats, and carbohydrates to create a balanced and appealing texture.

In recent years, there has been a rise in the popularity of grain-free and boutique dog foods that emphasize novel carbohydrate sources. While these diets cater to specific consumer preferences and perceived benefits, it's essential to approach them with a critical eye. The FDA has raised concerns about a potential link between specific grain-free diets and dilated cardiomyopathy (DCM), a severe heart condition, particularly in breeds not previously known to be predisposed to the disease. As research continues, dog owners are advised to consult with veterinarians to make informed choices about their pet's diet.

Carbohydrates also play a role in weight management for dogs. With the increasing prevalence of obesity in dogs, maintaining an appropriate balance of carbohydrates in the diet becomes crucial. High-fiber, low-calorie carbohydrates can contribute to a feeling of fullness, reducing the overall caloric intake and supporting weight loss efforts. Conversely, highly active dogs or those with higher energy requirements may benefit from diets with slightly higher carbohydrate content to meet their energy needs.

Understanding the glycemic index of carbohydrates is another consideration in optimizing a dog's diet. The glycemic index measures how quickly a carbohydrate source raises blood sugar levels. Low-glycemic carbohydrates, such as sweet potatoes and lentils, release glucose gradually, providing a sustained energy source and avoiding spikes in blood sugar. This can be particularly beneficial for dogs with diabetes or those at risk of developing insulin resistance.

In conclusion, beneficial carbohydrates are vital to a well-balanced and nutritious diet for dogs. From providing essential energy for their active lifestyles to supporting digestive health through fiber, carbohydrates contribute to various aspects of canine well-being. Whether it's whole grains or something else entirely, the selection of carbs should be made with the needs and sensitivities of each dog in mind. As our understanding of canine nutrition continues to evolve, so too does our ability to tailor diets that incorporate beneficial carbohydrates, ensuring the health and happiness of our beloved canine companions.

## Healthy Fats

In the dynamic realm of nutrition, the significance of dietary fats has undergone a paradigm shift, with a growing emphasis on the distinction between healthy and unhealthy fats. The discourse surrounding fats has transcended the conventional narrative of avoidance, as researchers and health professionals have come to recognize the pivotal role that healthy fats play in fostering overall well-being. This section explores the multifaceted dimensions of healthy fats, elucidating their sources, physiological benefits, and implications for human health.

The distinction between unsaturated and saturated fats is at the core of understanding healthy fats. Unsaturated fats often heralded as the "good" fats encompass both monounsaturated and polyunsaturated fats. Olive oil, avocados, and nuts are exemplary sources of monounsaturated fats, renowned for their heart-protective properties. Meanwhile, polyunsaturated fats in fatty fish, flaxseeds, and walnuts boast omega-3 and omega-6 fatty acids that are integral for brain function and inflammation regulation.

Contrastingly, saturated fats, predominant in animal-derived products such as red meat and dairy, have been associated with adverse health effects, particularly cardiovascular diseases. The intricate interplay between these contrasting types of fats underscores the importance of maintaining a balanced diet that tilts towards unsaturated fats to optimize health outcomes.

One noteworthy subset of polyunsaturated fats is omega-3 fatty acids, celebrated for their anti-inflammatory attributes. Fatty fish like salmon, mackerel, and sardines emerge as prominent sources of omega-3s, playing a crucial role in cardiovascular health, cognitive function, and mood regulation. Including these healthy fats in one's diet is emblematic of a holistic approach to nutrition, intertwining physical and mental well-being.

Beyond their cardiovascular benefits, healthy fats contribute significantly to the structural integrity of cell membranes, facilitating the efficient transport of nutrients and the expulsion of waste products. The intricate dance of lipids within our cellular framework underscores dietary fats' profound impact on cellular health, transcending their conventional role as mere energy sources.

Olive oil, often championed as a cornerstone of the Mediterranean diet, encapsulates the essence of healthy monounsaturated fats. Its antioxidant properties not only combat oxidative stress but also confer anti-inflammatory benefits. The symbiotic relationship between olive oil and cardiovascular health has been corroborated by extensive research, emphasizing the pivotal role that culinary choices can play in shaping our physiological well-being.

While the discourse on healthy fats predominantly revolves around their cardiovascular benefits, their influence on metabolic health is equally profound. Contrary to the traditional narrative associating fat intake with weight gain, research suggests that incorporating healthy fats into one's diet may aid in weight management. The satiating effect of fats and their ability to regulate blood sugar levels render them pivotal in curbing excessive caloric intake and promoting metabolic equilibrium.

Often lauded as a nutritional powerhouse, Avocado exemplifies the amalgamation of health-promoting compounds found in healthy fats. Beyond its monounsaturated fat content, avocados boast an array of vitamins, minerals, and fiber, accentuating their status as a superfood. Incorporating avocados into the diet transcends the conventional notion of fats as passive energy reservoirs, transforming them into active agents of nutritional fortification.

The ramifications of an imbalanced fat profile extend beyond the physiological realm, infiltrating the intricate tapestry of mental health. Emerging evidence suggests that omega-3 fatty acids, in particular, play a crucial role in cognitive function and mood regulation. The delicate balance of these essential fats in the brain underscores the interconnectedness of nutritional choices and mental well-being, shattering the dichotomy between physical and psychological health.

In the pursuit of optimizing fat intake for health, food preparation becomes a pivotal determinant. Grilled or baked preparations of fish, for instance, preserve the integrity of healthy fats, ensuring that the nutritional benefits are not compromised through the cooking process. Conversely, the excessive use of saturated and trans fats in frying and deep-frying methods exacerbates the health risks associated with these fats, underscoring the importance of mindful culinary practices.

The ubiquitous nature of fats in our diet necessitates a nuanced understanding of their impact on health. Food labeling and nutritional education are potent tools in empowering individuals to make informed dietary choices. The delineation between trans fats, saturated fats, and healthier counterparts becomes indispensable in fostering a society aware of dietary habits' profound influence on long-term health outcomes.

In conclusion, the narrative surrounding healthy fats transcends the simplistic dichotomy of good versus evil, delving into the intricate web of physiological, metabolic, and mental health dimensions. By embracing the essence of healthy fats through a diversified and balanced diet, individuals can cultivate a holistic approach to nutrition that fosters well-being across the spectrum. The journey towards optimal health intertwines with our conscientious choices in our dietary patterns, positioning healthy fats as essential allies in pursuing a vibrant and fulfilling life.

## Vitamins and Minerals

In the intricate tapestry of human nutrition, the significance of vitamins and minerals stands as an indomitable force, orchestrating a symphony of biochemical reactions that sustain life. These micronutrients, often relegated to the background of dietary discourse, are the unsung heroes that play a pivotal role in maintaining health and preventing many diseases. This section unravels the multifaceted world of vitamins and minerals, shedding light on their sources, functions, and profound implications for human well- being.

Vitamins, classified as water-soluble or fat-soluble, are organic compounds that the body requires in minute amounts for optimal functioning. Water-soluble vitamins, including the B-complex and vitamin C, are vital in energy metabolism, DNA synthesis, and immune function. The abundance of B vitamins in whole grains, legumes, and leafy greens underscores their role in cellular energy production. At the same time, citrus fruits and bell peppers stand as potent sources of vitamin C, known for their antioxidant prowess and immune-boosting capabilities.

Conversely, fat-soluble vitamins—A, D, E, and K—find solace in lipid-rich environments, necessitating dietary fat for optimal absorption. Vitamin A, abundant in orange and yellow fruits and vegetables, is integral for vision, immune function, and skin health. Vitamin D, often dubbed the "sunshine vitamin," is synthesized in the skin in response to sunlight exposure and is crucial for calcium absorption and bone health. Nuts, seeds, and vegetable oils offer a rich trove of vitamin E, an antioxidant that safeguards cells from oxidative damage. Vitamin K, found in leafy greens and cruciferous vegetables, plays a pivotal role in blood clotting and bone metabolism.

On the other hand, minerals are inorganic elements that the body requires for many physiological processes. Calcium, a cornerstone mineral, is integral for bone health and contributes to muscle function and blood clotting. Dairy products, leafy greens, and fortified foods emerge as robust sources of calcium, emphasizing the diversity of dietary avenues through which minerals can be obtained.

Magnesium, nestled within nuts, seeds, and whole grains, is an unsung hero in muscle and nerve function, energy metabolism, and bone health. Iron in animal and plant sources is indispensable for oxygen transport in the blood and preventing anemia. The intricate dance of minerals extends to zinc, a catalyst for immune function and wound healing, found abundantly in meat, dairy, and legumes.

While the macronutrients—carbohydrates, proteins, and fats—garner more attention, the micronutrients, vitamins, and minerals serve as the scaffolding upon which the foundation of human health is built. The harmonious interplay between these micronutrients is akin to a delicate ballet, each playing a specific role in ensuring the seamless functioning of physiological processes.

In the context of modern dietary patterns, fortified foods and supplements have become ubiquitous sources of vitamins and minerals. While these interventions may be necessary in deficiency cases, the synergistic relationships between nutrients in whole foods are unparalleled. Whole foods offer a symphony of vitamins and minerals, each complementing the other to create a robust and interconnected nutritional profile that cannot be replicated through isolated supplements.

The realm of vitamins and minerals extends its influence far beyond the confines of individual health, resonating with global health disparities and public health initiatives. Micronutrient deficiencies, often dubbed "hidden hunger," afflict populations worldwide, impeding growth, cognitive development, and immune function. Fortification programs, championed by public health agencies, seek to address these deficiencies by enriching staple foods with essential vitamins and minerals, offering a beacon of hope in the fight against malnutrition.

The delicate balance of vitamins and minerals extends to their impact on chronic diseases as protective agents and potential contributors to pathogenesis. Antioxidant vitamins, such as vitamins C and E, protect against oxidative stress, which is implicated in the aging process and the development of chronic diseases. Conversely, excessive intake of certain minerals, such as sodium, has been linked to hypertension and cardiovascular diseases, underscoring the importance of moderation in nutrient intake.

The dynamic nature of vitamins and minerals becomes particularly salient during specific life stages, such as pregnancy and old age. Pregnancy demands an augmented intake of vitamins and minerals, such as folic acid and iron, to support fetal development and prevent neural tube defects. In the twilight years, the body's ability to absorb certain nutrients diminishes, necessitating a more vigilant approach to nutrient intake through dietary choices or supplementation.

Dietary choices and culinary practices are potent determinants in assimilating vitamins and minerals. Cooking methods, food pairings, and the overall composition of meals influence the bioavailability of these micronutrients. For instance, the iron in plant-based foods is better absorbed in the presence of vitamin C-rich foods, exemplifying the intricate web of nutrient interactions that characterize the nutritional landscape.

In conclusion, the world of vitamins and minerals is a captivating tapestry woven into the fabric of human health. Their roles extend beyond the confines of individual nutrients, intertwining with physiological, global, and public health considerations. As we navigate the complexities of dietary choices, understanding the profound impact that vitamins and minerals exert on our well-being empowers us to make informed decisions, fostering a holistic approach to nutrition that resonates with the innate symphony of our bodies.

## Supplements for Optimal Canine Health

In the realm of canine care, the pursuit of optimal health for our four-legged companions is a shared goal among pet owners and veterinarians. Amidst the myriad of considerations, the role of supplements in promoting canine well-being emerges as a topic of growing interest and scrutiny. This section seeks to unravel the complexities surrounding the use of supplements for optimal canine health, delving into their potential benefits, considerations, and the evolving landscape of nutritional support for our beloved pets.

Like humans, the foundation of canine health lies in a well-balanced and nutritious diet. While commercial dog foods are formulated to meet the basic nutritional requirements, the diversity of canine breeds, sizes, and individual health conditions often necessitates a nuanced approach. This is where supplements come into play, serving as adjuncts to the regular diet to address specific needs and support overall health.

One of the primary categories of canine supplements encompasses vitamins and minerals. Just as in human nutrition, these micronutrients play pivotal roles in the physiological processes of dogs. However, unlike humans, dogs can synthesize their vitamin C, rendering supplementation unnecessary in most cases. Nevertheless, certain breeds, such as Bulldogs and Boxers, may benefit from vitamin C supplementation to support joint health and immune function.

Minerals, including calcium, phosphorus, and magnesium, are crucial for canine bone health. Puppies, in particular, require a balanced intake of these minerals to support proper skeletal development. Calcium supplements may be recommended for large breeds prone to skeletal issues. At the same time, older dogs may benefit from joint supplements containing glucosamine and chondroitin to maintain mobility and mitigate the effects of arthritis.

Omega-3 fatty acids from fish oil have gained prominence in canine supplementation. These essential fatty acids promote healthy skin and coat, reduce inflammation, and support cognitive function. Dogs with allergies, inflammatory conditions, or dry, flaky skin may find relief through omega-3 supplementation. However, it is essential to strike a balance, as excessive omega-3 intake can lead to unintended consequences, such as gastrointestinal upset.

The symbiotic relationship between gut health and overall well-being is not exclusive to humans; it also extends to our canine companions. Probiotics, live microorganisms that confer health benefits when administered in adequate amounts, have garnered attention for their potential to promote digestive health in dogs. Whether in the form of commercial supplements or naturally fermented foods, probiotics can aid in maintaining a healthy balance of gut flora, alleviating issues such as diarrhea, irritable bowel syndrome (IBS), and food sensitivities.

Joint health is critical to canine vitality, particularly in aging or large-breed dogs prone to arthritis and joint-related issues. Glucosamine and chondroitin supplements, often combined with other ingredients like MSM (methylsulfonylmethane), aim to support joint function, alleviate pain, and slow the progression of common degenerative diseases. However, the efficacy of these supplements is subject to variability, and consultation with a veterinarian is advised to determine the most suitable course of action based on the dog's needs.

Canine dietary needs extend beyond the basics, encompassing specialized supplements to address specific health concerns. For instance, dogs with anxiety or behavioral issues may benefit from supplements containing calming agents like L-theanine or chamomile. Similarly, antioxidants such as vitamins E and C and certain herbal extracts are touted for their potential to support canine cognitive function and stave off age-related cognitive decline.

As with any aspect of healthcare, supplements for canine health warrant a discerning and informed approach. The burgeoning market for pet supplements introduces myriad choices, each accompanied by its claims and promises. While the intent is to enhance the well-being of our furry companions, not all supplements are created equal. The quality of ingredients, dosage accuracy, and the manufacturer's reputation should be considered when selecting dog supplements.

Moreover, the adage "too much of a good thing" holds in canine supplementation. Excessive intake of specific vitamins and minerals can lead to toxicity and adverse effects. For instance, an overdose of vitamin D can result in hypercalcemia, causing symptoms like vomiting, weakness, and, in severe cases, kidney damage. Pet owners must adhere to recommended dosage guidelines and seek guidance from veterinarians to ensure that supplementation aligns with their dogs' specific needs and health status.

The landscape of canine nutrition is not static; it evolves alongside advancements in veterinary science and our understanding of the intricate nuances of canine health. Emerging trends in the field of supplements include the integration of natural and holistic approaches. Herbal supplements, such as turmeric for its anti-inflammatory properties or milk thistle for liver support, have gained traction among pet owners seeking alternative or complementary options to conventional treatments.

The conversation around canine health supplements also intersects with the broader discourse on the quality of commercial pet foods. As pet owners become increasingly conscious of ingredients and nutritional value, the demand for high-quality, nutritionally dense dog foods has surged. Supplements, therefore, become a strategic tool to bridge potential nutritional gaps in commercially available diets, ensuring that dogs receive a comprehensive array of essential nutrients.

In conclusion, the realm of supplements for optimal canine health is dynamic and nuanced. As devoted caretakers of our furry companions, it is incumbent upon us to navigate this terrain with diligence and a commitment to the well-being of our dogs. The judicious use of supplements, in conjunction with a balanced and nutritious diet, can contribute to our canine friends' longevity, vitality, and happiness, cementing our shared journey towards fostering the healthiest and happiest lives for man's best friend.

# CHAPTER III

# Basic Kitchen Tools and Equipment

## Must-Have Tools for Dog Food Preparation

In the realm of responsible pet ownership, providing our canine companions with nutritious and well-prepared meals is a cornerstone of their overall health and well-being. As the trend towards homemade dog food gains momentum, the importance of having the right tools for canine culinary endeavors becomes increasingly apparent. This section explores the must-have tools for dog food preparation, delving into the practicalities, considerations, and the symbiotic relationship between the tools we use and the quality of the meals we craft for our beloved pets.

A fundamental tool in the arsenal of canine cuisine is a reliable set of kitchen utensils, designed to streamline the preparation process and ensure the optimal nutritional value of the meals. Stainless steel bowls, designated for dog food use, are not only durable but also easy to clean, minimizing the risk of bacterial contamination. Measuring cups and spoons become essential in accurately portioning ingredients, facilitating precision in meeting a dog's dietary requirements. Additionally, a variety of cutting boards, separate from those used for human food preparation, contribute to maintaining hygiene and preventing cross-contamination.

The role of protein in a dog's diet cannot be overstated, and the tools used for handling and preparing meat become paramount. A sturdy set of kitchen shears proves invaluable for trimming fat and portioning meat, ensuring that the canine diet is rich in quality protein without unnecessary additives. A reliable meat grinder opens up possibilities for creating custom blends of protein sources, catering to the unique dietary needs and preferences of individual dogs. These tools empower pet owners to control the quality and composition of the protein component, fostering a holistic approach to canine nutrition.

Vegetables and fruits contribute essential vitamins and minerals to a dog's diet, and tools that facilitate their preparation play a crucial role in crafting well-rounded meals. A vegetable peeler and a reliable chef's knife become indispensable in processing a variety of vegetables, while a food processor or blender enables the creation of purees and mixes that can be seamlessly integrated into dog food recipes. The ability to finely chop or puree vegetables enhances their digestibility and absorption, unlocking the nutritional potential of plant-based ingredients for canine consumption.

In the pursuit of crafting balanced and wholesome meals, carbohydrates often play a supporting role in a dog's diet. Tools for processing grains and starches, such as rice, oats, or sweet potatoes, become essential. A rice cooker, for instance, simplifies the preparation of grains, ensuring that they are cooked to an ideal consistency for canine consumption. Food dehydrators offer a convenient method for creating homemade dog treats, utilizing a variety of fruits and vegetables to add both flavor and nutritional value to a dog's diet.

The importance of proper storage cannot be overlooked in the context of canine food preparation. Airtight containers safeguard the freshness and nutritional integrity of ingredients, preventing spoilage and bacterial contamination. Portion-sized containers facilitate meal planning, allowing pet owners to prepare and store individual servings, streamlining the feeding process and minimizing waste. Additionally, freezer-safe storage bags or containers become essential when preparing larger batches of homemade dog food, providing a convenient solution for preserving meals over an extended period.

While many canine diets focus on fresh and whole foods, the inclusion of certain supplements may be necessary to meet specific nutritional requirements. Tools for administering supplements, such as pill pockets or pill dispensers, prove invaluable for pet owners seeking a seamless way to incorporate essential vitamins or medications into their dog's meals. The ability to administer supplements effectively contributes to the overall success of a homemade diet tailored to a dog's individual needs.

The landscape of canine nutrition is ever-evolving, and the tools for dog food preparation extend beyond traditional kitchen utensils. The emergence of specialized appliances designed for crafting canine cuisine reflects the growing dedication of pet owners to providing the best possible nutrition for their dogs. Dog food processors, equipped with features tailored to canine dietary needs, streamline the preparation process by allowing pet owners to grind, mix, and blend ingredients with ease, creating customized meals that cater to the unique nutritional requirements of individual dogs.

Canine nutrition also intersects with the realm of technological advancements, as pet owners leverage online platforms and apps to access recipes, meal plans, and nutritional information. The digital age introduces a new dimension to the tools available for dog food preparation, offering a wealth of information and resources that empower pet owners to make informed decisions about their dog's diet. Mobile applications dedicated to canine nutrition provide a convenient means of accessing recipes, tracking dietary preferences, and staying informed about the latest developments in the field.

In conclusion, the tools for dog food preparation are instrumental in the journey towards crafting nutritious, well-balanced meals for our canine companions. From traditional kitchen utensils to specialized appliances and digital resources, each tool plays a role in shaping the quality of the food we provide for our dogs. The commitment to canine culinary excellence extends beyond the act of preparation; it is a testament to the profound bond between pet owners and their dogs, epitomizing the dedication to their health, happiness, and overall well-being. As we embark on the culinary adventure of crafting meals for our four-legged friends, the right tools become our allies, enriching the experience and contributing to the vitality of our cherished canine companions.

## Tips for Efficient and Safe Cooking

In the dynamic realm of culinary arts, the journey from amateur enthusiast to seasoned chef is marked by a commitment to mastering the art of efficient and safe cooking. The kitchen, often regarded as the heart of a home, becomes a stage where creativity and technique converge. This section aims to explore a compendium of tips that not only enhance the efficiency of cooking but also prioritize safety in the culinary process, fostering a harmonious and rewarding experience for individuals navigating the diverse landscape of the kitchen.

Efficiency in the kitchen begins with thoughtful

organization and preparation. Prior to commencing any culinary endeavor, take the time to gather all necessary ingredients and equipment. A mise en place not only streamlines the cooking process but also minimizes the risk of oversights, ensuring that every component of a recipe is readily available. This proactive approach lays the foundation for a seamless cooking experience, allowing the focus to shift to the artistry of combining flavors and textures.

Time management plays a pivotal role in efficient cooking.

Embrace the concept of multitasking, dividing tasks strategically to maximize productivity. Utilize downtime, such as waiting for water to boil or the oven to preheat, to complete preparatory steps or tidy up the workspace. This orchestration of tasks not only accelerates the cooking process but also instills a sense of rhythm and control in the kitchen, transforming it into a space of creative expression.

The judicious selection and maintenance of kitchen tools contribute significantly to cooking efficiency. Invest in high-quality knives and keep them sharp to facilitate precise and swift cutting. Familiarize yourself with the various utensils at your disposal, recognizing their unique functions and employing them strategically. Additionally, cultivate the habit of cleaning as you go, minimizing clutter and optimizing workspace for continued productivity.

Temperature management is a cornerstone of efficient cooking. Familiarize yourself with your stove and oven, understanding the nuances of heat distribution and responsiveness. Preheat the oven adequately, and when cooking on the stovetop, adjust the flame to match the specific needs of each dish. This mindfulness toward temperature ensures that ingredients cook uniformly, producing optimal textures and flavors.

Efficient cooking extends beyond the physical aspects of the kitchen to the conceptual realm of meal planning. Embrace batch cooking and meal prepping as strategies to optimize time and resources. Prepare larger quantities of staple ingredients, such as grains, proteins, and sauces, and store them for later use. This not only expedites subsequent meals but also provides a buffer for days when time is scarce.

While efficiency is paramount in the kitchen, it must coexist harmoniously with safety. The kitchen is a dynamic environment with inherent risks, and prioritizing safety measures is non-negotiable. Begin by familiarizing yourself with the layout of your kitchen, identifying potential hazards and ensuring that fire extinguishers and first aid kits are easily accessible. Implementing basic safety measures, such as securing loose cords and keeping flammable materials away from heat sources, establishes a foundation for accident prevention.

Proper knife handling is an essential facet of kitchen safety. Invest time in honing knife skills and adopt a grip that ensures control and precision. Regularly sharpen knives to maintain their efficacy, as dull blades are more prone to slips and accidents. When not in use, store knives securely and consider using blade guards to protect both the blades and the individuals handling them.

Understanding and managing heat sources are critical components of kitchen safety. Ensure that pot handles are turned inward on the stovetop to prevent accidental knocks or spills. Be mindful of hot surfaces and use oven mitts or pot holders to handle hot cookware. Invest in quality heat-resistant utensils to minimize the risk of burns and prioritize caution when working with open flames, such as those from gas stoves or grills.

Maintaining a clean and organized kitchen environment contributes significantly to safety. Regularly clean spills and crumbs to prevent slips and falls, and promptly store unused equipment to avoid unnecessary clutter. Establish a system for waste disposal, keeping trash bins away from heat sources to mitigate fire risks. Moreover, cultivate the habit of washing hands frequently to prevent cross-contamination and the spread of foodborne illnesses.

In the pursuit of culinary excellence, it is imperative to be cognizant of food safety practices. Adhere to recommended storage guidelines, refrigerating perishable items promptly, and discarding expired or spoiled ingredients. Thoroughly wash fruits and vegetables to remove contaminants, and employ separate cutting boards for raw meat, poultry, and produce to prevent cross-contamination. Familiarize yourself with safe minimum internal cooking temperatures for various proteins, ensuring that meals are not only delectable but also safe for consumption.

The efficient and safe cooking journey extends to the realm of food preparation and handling. Properly wash and sanitize cutting boards, utensils, and countertops to eliminate bacteria and prevent foodborne illnesses. Cultivate the habit of tasting dishes with clean utensils rather than double-dipping, reducing the risk of contamination. Additionally, use reputable sources for culinary knowledge, especially when experimenting with new recipes or techniques, to minimize the likelihood of unsafe practices.

In the age of technology, the culinary landscape has witnessed the integration of innovative tools that further enhance both efficiency and safety in the kitchen. Smart kitchen appliances, such as programmable sous-vide devices and precision cookers, offer precise temperature control, ensuring that dishes are cooked to perfection without the risk of overcooking. Additionally, kitchen thermometers equipped with Bluetooth connectivity provide real-time temperature monitoring, adding an extra layer of safety when preparing dishes that require specific temperature thresholds.

In conclusion, the mastery of efficient and safe cooking is an evolving journey that requires a synthesis of skill, knowledge, and mindfulness. The kitchen, often regarded as a canvas for culinary creativity, becomes a space where efficiency and safety dance in tandem, allowing individuals to express their passion for cooking without compromising well-being. By embracing organizational strategies, implementing safety measures, and leveraging technology, individuals can transform their kitchen into a haven of culinary artistry where efficiency and safety converge seamlessly, making every culinary endeavor a gratifying and secure experience.

## Storage Solutions for Homemade Dog Food

As the trend towards preparing homemade dog food gains traction, the importance of effective storage solutions becomes a paramount consideration in the overall canine culinary process. Crafting nutritious and wholesome meals for our four-legged friends is a labor of love, and ensuring the longevity and freshness of these homemade creations is equally crucial. This section explores a range of storage solutions tailored to the unique requirements of homemade dog food, delving into considerations, best practices, and the symbiotic relationship between proper storage and the well-being of our canine companions.

Understanding the nature of homemade dog food is essential when determining the most suitable storage methods. Unlike commercial dog food with preservatives, homemade meals often lack the additives that extend shelf life. Consequently, it is imperative to adopt storage practices that mitigate the risk of spoilage and bacterial contamination. Recognizing that ingredients such as meat, vegetables, and grains have varying storage needs is the first step in tailoring storage solutions to the specific components of homemade dog food.

A cornerstone of effective storage for homemade dog food is refrigeration. Refrigerators act as a fortress against the proliferation of harmful bacteria, slowing down the enzymatic reactions that lead to spoilage. When refrigerating homemade dog food, it is imperative to use airtight containers to prevent the absorption of odors from other foods and to maintain freshness. Portioning the food into smaller containers also allows for easy retrieval and minimizes the need to expose the entire batch to air each time the dog is fed.

For those who opt for batch cooking to streamline the canine culinary process, freezing emerges as a powerful ally in preserving homemade dog food. Freezing effectively halts bacterial growth and enzymatic reactions, extending the shelf life of meals. Invest in high-quality, freezer-safe containers or use vacuum-sealed bags to minimize the risk of freezer burn and maintain the nutritional integrity of the food. Labeling containers with the date of preparation ensures a systematic approach to utilizing frozen batches, preventing unnecessary waste.

Consideration for the type of ingredients used in homemade dog food is integral to proper storage. Ingredients with higher moisture content, such as cooked vegetables, may contribute to an environment conducive to bacterial growth. In such cases, it is advisable to prioritize refrigeration over room temperature storage. On the other hand, dehydrated or freeze-dried ingredients, common in many homemade dog food recipes, lend themselves well to room temperature storage, provided they are stored in a cool, dry place away from direct sunlight.

The containers chosen for storing homemade dog food play a crucial role in maintaining its quality. Airtight containers with secure seals act as guardians against air and moisture, preventing the infiltration of contaminants and preserving freshness. Opt for containers made from materials that do not leach harmful chemicals into the food, ensuring the safety of the canine diet. Transparent containers offer the added advantage of easy monitoring, allowing pet owners to assess the quantity and condition of stored food at a glance.

Homemade dog food often incorporates a variety of ingredients, each with its unique storage needs. Recognizing these nuances contributes to an informed approach to storage. Meats, for instance, should be stored in the refrigerator or freezer promptly after cooking to prevent the growth of harmful bacteria. Grains and starches, commonly used in canine recipes, benefit from a cool, dry storage environment to prevent moisture-induced spoilage. By categorizing ingredients based on their storage requirements, pet owners can adopt a targeted and effective approach to preserving the nutritional quality of homemade dog food.

When exploring storage solutions for homemade dog food, pet owners should be mindful of the storage duration. Unlike commercial dog food with specified expiration dates, homemade meals have a finite shelf life. A general guideline is to refrigerate or freeze homemade dog food within two hours of preparation to minimize the risk of bacterial contamination. Frozen batches of homemade dog food are typically safe for consumption for up to three months, while refrigerated portions should be consumed within three to five days.

Portion control is a fundamental aspect of both storage and feeding practices for homemade dog food. By dividing larger batches into individual portions, pet owners not only facilitate efficient storage but also streamline the feeding process. This approach minimizes the frequency of exposing the entire batch to air, reducing the risk of contamination and spoilage. Additionally, portioning allows for easy customization of meals based on the size, age, and dietary needs of individual dogs.

In the realm of storage solutions, consider the environmental impact of the chosen containers and methods. Opting for reusable, eco-friendly containers aligns with a sustainable approach to pet care. Glass containers, for instance, are an environmentally conscious alternative to plastic and do not leach harmful chemicals. The conscientious selection of storage solutions contributes to a holistic approach to canine nutrition that considers both the well-being of our pets and the broader ecological footprint of our choices.

The evolution of canine nutrition is intertwined with advancements in technology, and storage solutions for homemade dog food are no exception. Smart storage containers equipped with vacuum-sealing capabilities or freshness indicators offer a technologically enhanced approach to preserving homemade dog food. These containers leverage innovation to extend shelf life, maintain optimal freshness, and provide pet owners with real-time information about the condition of stored food.

As the landscape of canine nutrition continues to evolve, the integration of technology extends beyond smart storage containers. Mobile applications and digital platforms dedicated to pet care provide pet owners with tools to streamline meal planning, monitor nutritional intake, and receive reminders for optimal storage durations. The digital age offers a wealth of resources that empower pet owners to navigate the intricacies of homemade dog food preparation and storage with precision.

In conclusion, storage solutions for homemade dog food are an integral component of responsible pet ownership. Crafting nutritious meals for our canine companions is an expression of love and commitment, and the preservation of these homemade creations demands thoughtful consideration. By aligning storage practices with the unique needs of homemade dog food, pet owners can ensure that every meal served is a testament to the dedication to the well-being of their cherished companions. The art of storing homemade dog food is an evolving journey, one that intertwines practicality, innovation, and a deep-seated commitment to providing our dogs with the best possible nutrition.

# CHAPTER IV

# Simple and Nutritious Breakfast Recipes

## Protein-Packed Breakfast Bowls

In the landscape of culinary wellness, breakfast emerges as the cornerstone of a nourishing start to the day. Among the myriad breakfast options available, protein- packed breakfast bowls have surged in popularity, captivating the taste buds of health enthusiasts and foodies alike. This section embarks on a flavorful journey through the realm of protein-packed breakfast bowls, exploring their nutritional merits, versatility, and the potential they hold for transforming mornings into a vibrant celebration of wholesome indulgence.

At the heart of the protein-packed breakfast bowl phenomenon lies the recognition of protein as an essential macronutrient with unparalleled nutritional significance. Proteins are the building blocks of the body, playing a pivotal role in muscle development, immune function, and the maintenance of healthy skin, hair, and nails. Incorporating a substantial amount of protein into the first meal of the day provides a sustained source of energy, curbing mid-morning cravings and stabilizing blood sugar levels—a key consideration for those navigating the demands of a bustling day.

The foundation of a protein-packed breakfast bowl typically revolves around diverse protein sources, offering individuals the flexibility to cater to personal preferences and dietary restrictions. Traditional options include eggs, dairy products, and lean meats, while plant-based alternatives like legumes, tofu, and quinoa cater to the growing demand for vegetarian and vegan breakfast options. This versatility ensures that protein-packed breakfast bowls can be tailored to accommodate various dietary philosophies, making them an inclusive and accessible choice for a wide array of individuals.

The evolution of breakfast bowls transcends the conventional confines of a single food category, embracing a symphony of ingredients that contribute to both flavor and nutritional density. Greek yogurt, renowned for its creamy texture and rich protein content, often serves as the anchor for many protein-packed breakfast bowls. Complemented by fresh fruits, nuts, and seeds, these bowls not only provide a delectable medley of textures and tastes but also deliver a diverse array of nutrients, including vitamins, minerals, and healthy fats.

Eggs, a perennial breakfast favorite, manifest in protein-packed breakfast bowls in various forms. Whether poached, scrambled, or boiled, eggs contribute a high-quality protein source that is easily digestible and satiating. Incorporating eggs into breakfast bowls opens the door to endless possibilities, as they harmonize effortlessly with an assortment of vegetables, herbs, and grains, creating a culinary canvas that appeals to both the palate and the nutritional requirements of the body.

The ascent of plant-based diets has ushered in a new era of protein-packed breakfast bowl innovation. Legumes, such as chickpeas and black beans, inject a hearty dose of protein, fiber, and micronutrients into breakfast bowls, offering a savory and satisfying alternative to animal-derived proteins. Tofu, celebrated for its versatility, absorbs the flavors of accompanying ingredients, making it a prized addition to plant-based breakfast bowls that defy expectations and showcase the artistry of plant-centric cooking.

Grains, often relegated to the sidelines, emerge as silent heroes in the realm of protein-packed breakfast bowls. Quinoa, with its complete protein profile, becomes a staple that imparts a nutty texture and an earthy flavor to breakfast creations. Oats, celebrated for their heart-healthy properties, serve as a canvas for sweet and savory combinations, marrying seamlessly with fruits, nuts, and yogurt to construct a protein-packed breakfast bowl that transcends traditional notions of oatmeal.

The art of constructing a protein-packed breakfast bowl lies not only in the selection of ingredients but also in the mindful orchestration of flavors and textures. Combining contrasting elements—such as crunchy nuts with creamy yogurt, sweet fruits with savory grains—creates a harmonious balance that elevates the breakfast experience. The layering of textures, from the silky smoothness of yogurt to the crispness of granola, transforms each spoonful into a sensory journey that captivates the senses and imparts a sense of indulgence to the morning routine.

The emergence of protein-packed breakfast bowls aligns with contemporary lifestyles that demand convenience without compromising on nutritional quality. The assembly of these bowls is characterized by simplicity and efficiency, making them an accessible option for individuals navigating busy mornings. Preparing components in advance, such as overnight oats or pre-chopped fruits and vegetables, streamlines the morning routine, allowing individuals to savor a nutrient-rich breakfast without sacrificing precious moments of repose.

Beyond the realm of nutrition, protein-packed breakfast bowls symbolize a departure from conventional breakfast norms, embodying a spirit of culinary creativity and self-expression. The act of assembling a personalized breakfast bowl becomes a canvas for innovation, encouraging individuals to experiment with unique flavor combinations, textures, and presentations. The morning ritual transforms into a culinary adventure, fostering a positive and energizing start to the day.

In the quest for optimal nutrition, the consideration of macronutrient balance becomes pivotal, and protein-packed breakfast bowls excel in achieving this equilibrium. The satiating power of protein, coupled with the sustained energy release it provides, contributes to improved appetite control throughout the day. For those on a journey of weight management or muscle building, the inclusion of protein-packed breakfast bowls becomes a strategic ally, offering a delicious and wholesome means of meeting daily protein requirements.

The influence of social media and culinary trends has played a pivotal role in catapulting protein-packed breakfast bowls into the spotlight. Instagram feeds abound with vibrant images of meticulously arranged bowls, adorned with a kaleidoscope of colors and textures that invite viewers into the realm of gastronomic artistry. Influencers and food enthusiasts alike share their renditions, inspiring a global audience to embrace the creativity and nutritional benefits inherent in the art of crafting protein-packed breakfast bowls.

The culinary landscape is ever-evolving, and the popularity of protein-packed breakfast bowls signifies a paradigm shift in breakfast culture. No longer confined to mundane and repetitive morning rituals, individuals are empowered to curate breakfast experiences that align with their unique tastes, preferences, and nutritional goals. The protein-packed breakfast bowl exemplifies the evolving narrative of breakfast, offering a canvas for culinary expression that celebrates health, flavor, and the joy of savoring a well-rounded start to the day.

In conclusion, protein-packed breakfast bowls stand as a testament to the intersection of nutrition, culinary innovation, and the evolving preferences of contemporary lifestyles. Beyond their nutritional prowess, these bowls embody the essence of a mindful and flavorful start to the day. Whether adorned with fruits, nuts, seeds, or savory elements, protein-packed breakfast bowls transcend mere sustenance, becoming a celebration of the culinary arts and a testament to the belief that nourishing the body can be a delightful and indulgent affair.

# Fruity Delights for Morning Energy

In the rhythmic cadence of mornings, the pursuit of energy-packed nourishment takes center stage, and the vibrant symphony of fruity delights emerges as a beacon of freshness and vitality. The inclusion of fruits in the morning routine not only tantalizes the taste buds but also infuses the body with a burst of natural sugars, essential vitamins, and hydrating fluids. This section embarks on a journey through the realm of fruity delights for morning energy, exploring their nutritional virtues, culinary versatility, and the transformative power they wield in elevating the dawn of a new day.

At the heart of the appeal of fruity delights lies the innate sweetness and juiciness that fruits bring to the breakfast table. Laden with natural sugars, fruits serve as nature's energy-packed candy, offering a delicious alternative to refined sugars and processed snacks. The consumption of fruits in the morning provides a quick and efficient source of energy, elevating blood sugar levels and kickstarting metabolic processes—an ideal foundation for a day of productivity and vitality.

The nutritional profile of fruits contributes to their status as morning superfoods. Rich in vitamins, minerals, and antioxidants, fruits play a crucial role in supporting overall health and well-being. Vitamin C, abundant in citrus fruits like oranges and grapefruits, boosts immune function, while potassium in bananas aids in maintaining electrolyte balance. The fiber content of fruits promotes digestive health and sustains feelings of fullness, curbing unnecessary snacking and promoting mindful eating habits throughout the day.

The versatility of fruits lends itself to a myriad of culinary possibilities, allowing individuals to tailor their morning indulgences to personal preferences and dietary goals. Fresh, whole fruits make for convenient and portable breakfast options, requiring minimal preparation. Sliced apples, a handful of berries, or a juicy mango can be enjoyed on their own or paired with yogurt, granola, or nut butter to create a customized and satisfying breakfast bowl that balances sweetness with protein and healthy fats.

The culinary canvas of fruity delights extends beyond simplicity to embrace the artistry of smoothie creation. Blending a medley of fruits with yogurt, milk, or plant-based alternatives transforms breakfast into a sensory experience that combines taste, texture, and nourishment. The addition of greens like spinach or kale introduces an extra layer of nutritional density, making morning smoothies a vibrant and wholesome choice for those seeking a delightful and energizing start to the day.

The amalgamation of fruits with whole grains and proteins amplifies their potential as morning energy boosters. Breakfast parfaits, layering fruits with Greek yogurt and granola, offer a harmonious blend of textures and flavors that satisfies both the palate and the body's nutritional needs. Overnight oats infused with fruits, nuts, and seeds present a convenient and customizable option that can be prepared in advance, streamlining the morning routine without compromising on nutrition.

Fruits also find their place in the realm of baked goods, adding natural sweetness and moisture to morning treats. Muffins, pancakes, and waffles can be infused with the succulence of berries, the warmth of cinnamon-spiced apples, or the tropical flair of diced pineapple. These fruity delights transcend the traditional boundaries of breakfast, offering a delightful fusion of wholesome ingredients that redefine the morning culinary experience.

The appeal of fruity delights extends beyond the nutritional and culinary realms to encompass the sensory experience they evoke. The vibrant colors, enticing aromas, and succulent textures of fruits engage the senses and create a multisensory breakfast ritual that transcends mere sustenance. The act of savoring a perfectly ripe piece of fruit becomes a moment of mindfulness, a pause in the bustling morning routine that allows individuals to connect with the present and relish the simple joys of nourishment.

In the pursuit of morning energy, the timing of fruit consumption plays a strategic role. While the sugars in fruits provide a quick energy boost, pairing them with slower-digesting proteins and fats ensures sustained energy release throughout the morning. Balancing a fruit-heavy breakfast with proteins such as Greek yogurt, cottage cheese, or a sprinkle of nuts offers a harmonious blend of macronutrients that stabilizes blood sugar levels and keeps hunger at bay, promoting a steady and enduring vitality.

The role of fruits in morning energy extends beyond the boundaries of the physical body to encompass mental clarity and focus. The natural sugars in fruits serve as a readily available energy source for the brain, enhancing cognitive function and alertness. The hydration provided by water-rich fruits contributes to overall mental well-being, preventing the cognitive sluggishness often associated with dehydration. As individuals embark on the day's tasks and challenges, the inclusion of fruity delights becomes a holistic approach to supporting both physical and mental vigor.

In the age of health-conscious living, the popularity of fruity delights for morning energy resonates with individuals seeking a balance between flavor and nutrition. Social media platforms abound with visually appealing images of fruit-filled breakfast bowls, smoothie creations, and colorful fruit platters, inspiring a global audience to embrace the vibrant and wholesome nature of fruity breakfasts. Influencers and wellness advocates alike extol the virtues of starting the day with nature's candy, creating a movement that celebrates the joy of morning nourishment.

As individuals weave fruity delights into their morning routines, the benefits extend to broader health outcomes. The antioxidants present in fruits contribute to cellular health, supporting the body's defense against oxidative stress and inflammation. The fiber content aids in digestion and promotes a healthy gut microbiome, influencing overall digestive well-being. The vitamins and minerals found in fruits play diverse roles, from supporting immune function to promoting bone health, underscoring the notion that morning energy is not merely a fleeting burst but a foundational investment in holistic health.

In conclusion, the allure of fruity delights for morning energy resides in their ability to seamlessly blend nutrition, flavor, and vitality. Beyond the natural sugars and vitamins, fruits offer a sensory and culinary experience that transforms breakfast into a moment of celebration and nourishment. Whether enjoyed in their whole, raw form or incorporated into an array of creative breakfast concoctions, fruity delights serve as ambassadors of morning energy, infusing the dawn of a new day with a symphony of freshness and vibrancy.

## Homemade Doggy Granola Bars

In the realm of responsible pet ownership, the quest for wholesome and nutritious treats for our canine companions takes center stage. As an alternative to commercially available dog treats with uncertain ingredients, homemade doggy granola bars have emerged as a popular choice among pet owners seeking to provide their furry friends with delectable and healthful indulgences. This section embarks on a flavorful exploration into the world of crafting homemade doggy granola bars, unraveling the nutritional benefits, ingredient considerations, and the joyous process of creating tail-wagging treats that epitomize the intersection of love and canine well-being.

The foundation of homemade doggy granola bars lies in the recognition of the nutritional needs of our canine friends. Dogs, like humans, benefit from a balanced diet that incorporates a variety of nutrients to support their overall health. Crafting treats at home allows pet owners to control the quality of ingredients, avoiding additives and preservatives commonly found in commercial dog treats. The choice of wholesome ingredients in homemade granola bars becomes a conscious decision to prioritize the well-being of our four-legged companions.

A key consideration in crafting homemade doggy granola bars is the selection of ingredients that are not only palatable but also safe for canine consumption. Rolled oats, a staple in many granola bar recipes, offer a source of whole grains and dietary fiber that aids in digestion. Peanut butter, a favorite among dogs, not only contributes to the irresistible flavor of the bars but also provides healthy fats and protein. The inclusion of fruits, such as apples or blueberries, introduces essential vitamins and antioxidants, enriching the nutritional profile of the treats.

The absence of certain ingredients commonly found in human granola bars is paramount when creating treats for dogs. While chocolate, raisins, and certain nuts are popular in human granola bars, they pose potential health risks to dogs. Chocolate contains theobromine, which is toxic to dogs, while raisins can lead to kidney damage. Nuts, especially macadamia nuts, can also be harmful. Homemade doggy granola bars prioritize canine-friendly ingredients, ensuring that each bite is not only delicious but also safe for consumption.

The process of crafting homemade doggy granola bars becomes a collaborative and joyous venture between pet owners and their dogs. The aromatic scent of baking fills the air as ingredients are mixed and shaped into bars, creating a sensory experience that engages both human and canine senses. The act of creating treats at home fosters a sense of connection and care, as pet owners tailor recipes to suit the individual preferences and dietary needs of their beloved companions.

Homemade doggy granola bars present an opportunity for customization, allowing pet owners to cater to the specific dietary requirements and taste preferences of their dogs. The incorporation of protein sources, such as lean meats or eggs, enhances the nutritional value of the bars, supporting muscle development and overall canine health. Experimenting with different flavors, textures, and ingredient combinations becomes a culinary adventure, with each batch of granola bars tailored to the unique palate of the individual dog.

Nutritional balance in homemade doggy granola bars is achieved through a thoughtful combination of ingredients that mirror the components of a well-rounded canine diet. The inclusion of protein-rich ingredients, such as eggs or lean meats, ensures that the treats contribute to the daily protein intake necessary for muscle maintenance and energy. Healthy fats from ingredients like peanut butter or coconut oil provide a source of energy and contribute to a shiny coat. The addition of fruits and vegetables introduces essential vitamins and minerals that support immune function and overall well-being.

Beyond the nutritional benefits, the act of presenting homemade doggy granola bars becomes an expression of love and consideration for a furry family member. The ritual of offering a freshly baked treat signifies a moment of connection and joy between pet owner and dog. The tail-wagging excitement and appreciative glances exchanged during treat time create a bond that extends beyond the culinary realm, embodying the mutual affection and companionship shared between humans and their dogs.

In the landscape of pet care, the awareness of food allergies and sensitivities among dogs underscores the importance of homemade doggy granola bars. Commercial treats often contain fillers, additives, and potential allergens that may contribute to digestive discomfort or allergic reactions in some dogs. Crafting treats at home allows pet owners to tailor recipes to accommodate specific dietary restrictions, ensuring that each granola bar is a safe and enjoyable indulgence for dogs with sensitivities.

The nutritional integrity of homemade doggy granola bars is further enhanced by the absence of artificial additives and preservatives commonly found in commercial dog treats. The reliance on natural, whole-food ingredients translates to treats that are free from unnecessary fillers and artificial colors. The transparency in ingredient selection empowers pet owners to make informed choices about the treats they offer to their dogs, aligning with a commitment to providing the best possible nutrition for their canine companions.

The versatility of homemade doggy granola bars extends beyond traditional baking to accommodate a variety of dietary preferences and restrictions. For dogs with grain sensitivities, recipes can be adapted to include alternative flours such as coconut or chickpea flour. For dogs following a vegetarian or vegan diet, ingredients like flaxseed or chia seeds can be incorporated to enhance the nutritional content without compromising on flavor. The adaptability of recipes allows pet owners to create treats that align with the specific dietary philosophy guiding their dog's nutrition.

In the context of canine health, the portion control facilitated by homemade doggy granola bars contributes to a mindful approach to treat-giving. The ability to customize the size and shape of the bars allows pet owners to manage calorie intake, especially for dogs with weight management considerations. Portioning treats according to the size and breed of the dog ensures that each treat is a delightful indulgence without compromising the overall balance of the canine diet.

The rising popularity of homemade doggy granola bars aligns with the broader movement towards mindful and personalized pet care. As pet owners seek to provide their dogs with nutrition that mirrors their own commitment to health and well-being, the act of crafting treats at home becomes a natural extension of this ethos. Social media platforms abound with images of pet owners proudly presenting their homemade creations, inspiring a community of like-minded individuals to embrace the joy of homemade canine treats.

The journey of crafting homemade doggy granola bars transcends the realm of culinary arts to become a celebration of the bond between pet owner and dog. The shared experience of preparing treats at home fosters a sense of collaboration and communication, as dogs eagerly await the outcome of the baking process. The act of offering a homemade treat becomes a gesture of love, care, and the shared enjoyment of a delectable creation that symbolizes the deep connection between human and canine.

In conclusion, homemade doggy granola bars epitomize the intersection of culinary creativity, nutritional consciousness, and the expression of love for our canine companions. Beyond being a tasty indulgence, these treats embody the dedication of pet owners to the well-being and happiness of their dogs. The act of crafting treats at home is a journey filled with joy, customization, and the shared delight that emanates from presenting a tail-wagging creation that mirrors the love and devotion exchanged between humans and their furry friends.

# CHAPTER V

# Wholesome Lunch Ideas

## Hearty Meat and Vegetable Stews

In the rich tapestry of culinary delights, few dishes embody warmth, comfort, and wholesome satisfaction as effectively as hearty meat and vegetable stews. These savory concoctions, simmering with a medley of flavors and textures, represent a culinary tradition that transcends cultural boundaries and seasons. This section delves into the artistry of crafting hearty stews, exploring the nutritional merits, diverse culinary traditions, and the soul-soothing experience that emanates from each steaming bowl—a testament to the enduring appeal of this timeless comfort food.

The allure of hearty meat and vegetable stews lies in their ability to transform simple ingredients into a symphony of flavors that resonate with tradition and innovation. The foundation often comprises succulent cuts of meat—be it beef, lamb, poultry, or even game—whose slow and gentle cooking renders them tender and infused with the aromatic essence of the dish. Adding an assortment of vegetables, from root vegetables like carrots and potatoes to leafy greens and legumes, not only enhances the nutritional profile but also contributes to the robust texture and complexity of the stew.

Nutritional richness is a hallmark of hearty stews, making them a nourishing choice that aligns with the principles of a balanced diet. The slow-cooking process allows the flavors to meld while preserving the integrity of the ingredients. Including various vegetables introduces an array of essential vitamins, minerals, and dietary fiber, promoting digestive health and overall well-being. The protein from the meat source adds a satiating element, contributing to muscle maintenance and energy levels—a nutritional synergy that has sustained generations.

The global tapestry of culinary traditions is reflected in the diverse array of hearty stews that have found a cherished place in kitchens worldwide. From the iconic French Boeuf Bourguignon, simmered in red wine, to the Spanish Caldo Gallego, a hearty mix of greens and chorizo, each culture has woven its unique flavors into the fabric of this comforting dish. The Moroccan Tagine, the Italian Osso Buco, and the Japanese Nikujaga are all examples of how regional variations and creative cooking have turned the simple stew into a work of art.

Preparing hearty meat and vegetable stews invites a sensory journey that begins with the aromas wafting through the kitchen. The slow and deliberate process of building flavors, from searing meat to sautéing vegetables, creates a symphony of scents that permeates the air—a prelude to the soul-soothing experience awaiting those partaking in the final creation. The anticipation builds as the stew simmers, allowing the ingredients to meld into a harmonious blend that promises to satiate both hunger and the desire for culinary comfort.

The adaptability of hearty stews shines through in their ability to showcase local ingredients, seasonal produce, and culinary creativity. Whether it's the addition of root vegetables in the winter months, a burst of fresh herbs in the spring, or using regional spices to infuse a distinctive character, stews are a canvas for culinary expression. The flexibility in ingredient choices allows home cooks and chefs alike to tailor their stews to personal preferences, dietary considerations, and the availability of local produce.

In culinary arts, the slow-cooking method inherent in preparing hearty stews is an exercise in patience and precision. The long, slow simmering not only tenderizes the meat but also allows the flavors to intensify and meld. The skill lies in achieving the perfect balance—ensuring the stew is neither overcooked nor underdeveloped. This nuanced approach to cooking demands an understanding of ingredients, heat control, and the art of layering flavors, making the process as rewarding as the result.

The cultural and familial significance of hearty stews extends beyond their culinary appeal. Often rooted in tradition and passed down through generations, stew recipes become a repository of domestic history and culinary heritage. Preparing and sharing a hearty stew carries the weight of shared memories and the comfort derived from the continuity of culinary practices. Whether served during festive gatherings, family reunions, or as a nurturing meal during challenging times, hearty stews become a source of connection and continuity in the tapestry of familial traditions.

The ritual of serving hearty stews transcends the boundaries of the dining table to become a gesture of hospitality and communal sharing. The combined pot, simmering with savory goodness, invites loved ones to gather, savor, and share stories. Scooping out generous portions, often accompanied by a crusty loaf of bread or a bed of grains, fosters an atmosphere of friendliness and togetherness. In this shared experience, the stew becomes more than a meal—a conduit for fostering relationships and creating lasting memories.

The nutritional benefits of hearty stews extend beyond their comforting flavors to address contemporary dietary preferences and health-conscious lifestyles. The emphasis on lean cuts of meat, an abundance of vegetables, and the exclusion of excessive fats aligns with the principles of a balanced and mindful diet. The adaptability of stew recipes allows for incorporating plant-based proteins, catering to the growing demand for vegetarian and vegan options. Hearty vegetable stews, enriched with legumes and grains, stand as a flavorful testament to the marriage of nutrition and culinary innovation.

In the modern culinary landscape, where time is often a precious commodity, the convenience of one-pot cooking has elevated hearty stews to a sought-after choice for busy individuals and families. The simplicity of preparation, the minimal need for supervision, and the potential for leftovers that often taste even better the next day make stews a practical and time-efficient option. Whether cooked on a stovetop, in a slow cooker, or in an instant pot, the adaptability of stew recipes accommodates the dynamic lifestyles of contemporary home cooks.

The nutritional density of hearty stews positions them as a strategic ally for those seeking a well-rounded and satisfying meal. The balance of macronutrients—protein, carbohydrates, and fats—offers sustained energy release, making stews an ideal choice for those with active lifestyles or athletes needing post-workout nourishment. Including nutrient-rich vegetables contributes to a diverse array of vitamins and minerals, supporting immune function and promoting overall health.

The evolving landscape of dietary preferences and culinary trends has ushered in creative adaptations of traditional hearty stews to meet the demands of diverse palates. Vegan and vegetarian variations featuring plant-based solid proteins like tofu, tempeh, or legumes showcase the culinary ingenuity of plant-centric cooking. Ethnic fusion stews, marrying flavors from different culinary traditions, provide a delightful twist that adds excitement and global inspiration to the classic stew experience.

In conclusion, the enduring appeal of hearty meat and vegetable stews resides in their ability to transcend time, cultural boundaries, and dietary trends. These comforting creations, simmering with tradition and innovation, exemplify the culinary arts as a source of nourishment, connection, and satisfaction. From the savory aroma that heralds their creation to the communal sharing that defines their consumption, hearty stews stand as a testament to the timeless allure of comfort food. This culinary symphony resonates with the universal desire for warmth, sustenance, and joy from a steaming bowl of soul-soothing goodness.

## Balanced Rice and Meat Lunch Bowls

In the dynamic landscape of contemporary culinary culture, the rise of balanced rice and meat lunch bowls has been nothing short of a gastronomic revolution. These thoughtfully crafted bowls, a harmonious marriage of grains, proteins, and an array of vibrant ingredients, exemplify the principles of balanced nutrition and culinary ingenuity. This section embarks on a flavorful exploration into the world of flat rice and meat lunch bowls, unraveling their nutritional significance, culinary diversity, and the sensory delight they bring to the table— a celebration of harmony in every delicious bite.

The commitment to nutritional balance is at the core of the appeal of balanced rice and meat lunch bowls. This delicate equilibrium ensures the body receives a spectrum of essential nutrients. Including grains, often rice, serves as a wholesome foundation, providing complex carbohydrates that serve as a sustained energy source. The protein component, derived from various meat sources, offers essential amino acids for muscle development, repair, and overall well-being. This marriage of macronutrients is satiating and aligns with contemporary dietary preferences that prioritize a balanced and mindful approach to eating.

The versatility of balanced rice and meat lunch bowls manifests in the diverse array of grains and proteins that can be incorporated. Brown rice, quinoa, bulgur, or farro are nutrient-rich alternatives to traditional white rice, contributing additional fiber, vitamins, and minerals. Similarly, proteins extend beyond conventional choices like chicken or beef to include seafood, tofu, or plant-based alternatives, catering to the evolving landscape of dietary preferences and culinary innovation. This adaptability ensures that lunch bowls can be tailored to meet individual tastes, dietary restrictions, and nutritional goals.

The nutritional richness of balanced rice and meat lunch bowls extends beyond the primary macronutrients to embrace a symphony of vitamins, minerals, and phytonutrients. Including a colorful medley of vegetables —from leafy greens and cruciferous varieties to vibrant bell peppers and tomatoes—infuses the bowls with a diverse array of antioxidants, promoting cellular health and bolstering the immune system. Fresh herbs, such as cilantro, basil, or mint, enhance flavor and contribute micronutrients with their own set of health benefits. The integration of healthy fats, sourced from ingredients like avocados, nuts, or olive oil, completes the nutritional ensemble, supporting cognitive function and nutrient absorption.

Culinary creativity takes center stage in constructing balanced rice and meat lunch bowls, offering a canvas for the artful assembly of flavors, textures, and visual appeal. The process begins with selecting grains, where the choice of rice or alternative grains sets the tone for the bowl. Whether grilled, roasted, or seared, proteins lend a savory depth to the ensemble. Various roasted, pickled, or raw veggies can add a pop of color and freshness, while toppings like cheese, almonds, or seeds can add interesting textures and flavors. Sauces and dressings, from tahini-based blends to zesty vinaigrettes, tie the components together, elevating the entire bowl into a delectable and cohesive culinary creation.

The global culinary tapestry is vividly represented in the myriad variations of balanced rice and meat lunch bowls that draw inspiration from diverse culinary traditions. The Japanese Chirashi Bowl, adorned with fresh sashimi atop a bed of sushi rice, showcases the delicate artistry of Japanese cuisine. The Mexican Burrito Bowl, marrying seasoned meats with black beans, rice, and vibrant salsas, brings the bold flavors of Mexican street food to the forefront. The Mediterranean Grain Bowl, featuring couscous or bulgur with grilled lamb or falafel, pays homage to the sun-drenched flavors of the Mediterranean. These bowls become vessels for cultural expression, embodying the essence of regional ingredients, preparation techniques, and culinary aesthetics.

The experience of savoring a balanced rice and meat lunch bowl is not merely a gustatory delight but a multisensory journey that engages sight, smell, and texture. The vibrant colors of fresh vegetables, the aromatic allure of grilled meats, and the contrasting textures of crunchy seeds or creamy avocados create a visual and olfactory spectacle that heightens the overall dining experience. Assembling and enjoying the bowl becomes a ritual that fosters a mindful connection with the food, inviting individuals to appreciate the diversity of flavors and the nutritional bounty within each carefully curated bite.

In dietary wellness, the concept of balance takes on added significance, and balanced rice and meat lunch bowls emerge as a strategic tool for achieving and maintaining nutritional equilibrium. Including lean proteins, whole grains, and a spectrum of vegetables aligns with dietary guidelines that promote heart health, weight management, and overall well-being. For individuals navigating specific nutritional needs—whether aiming for increased protein intake, adhering to a plant-based diet, or managing blood sugar levels—the adaptability of lunch bowls becomes a valuable ally in achieving nutritional goals without sacrificing culinary satisfaction.

The convenience and efficiency of balanced rice and meat lunch bowls align with the demands of modern lifestyles, offering a solution for individuals seeking wholesome and time-efficient meal options. The prep-ahead nature of many components—such as batch-cooked grains, grilled proteins, and pre-chopped vegetables—streamlines the assembly process, making lunch bowls an accessible choice for those with busy schedules. The portability of lunch bowls also caters to individuals on the go, allowing them to enjoy a nutritious and satisfying meal without compromising flavor or nutritional quality.

The culinary phenomenon of balanced rice and meat lunch bowls is not confined to home kitchens; it has permeated restaurant menus, cafes, and food establishments worldwide. The popularity of customizable bowl concepts, where patrons can select their preferred grains, proteins, vegetables, and toppings, reflects the widespread appeal of this culinary trend. The social media landscape further amplifies the trend, with Instagram feeds adorned with visually stunning images of vibrant lunch bowls that serve as culinary inspiration and celebrate wholesome, balanced eating.

The conscious effort to reduce food waste finds resonance in the adaptability of balanced rice and meat lunch bowls, where leftovers can be repurposed into creative and flavorful reincarnations. "bowl remixing" encourages individuals to reimagine and reinvent their lunch bowls by incorporating fresh components or experimenting with new flavor profiles. This approach not only minimizes food waste but also adds an element of culinary excitement to daily meals, fostering a sustainable and creative approach to eating.

In conclusion, the rise of balanced rice and meat lunch bowls symbolizes a culinary movement that harmonizes nutritional principles with diverse flavors, textures, and cultural influences. These bowls encapsulate the essence of modern dietary preferences, emphasizing balance, mindfulness, and culinary enjoyment. Whether savored at home, prepared with love in a family kitchen, or enjoyed at a bustling restaurant, the appeal of balanced rice and meat lunch bowls lies in their ability to transcend the boundaries of tradition, offering a dynamic and flavorful canvas that adapts to the evolving palate and nutritional goals of individuals worldwide.

## DIY Doggy Burgers for a Midday Treat

Treating our furry friends to culinary delights in the realm of pet care and canine companionship has evolved into a delightful and creative endeavor. Enter the world of DIY doggy burgers—a canine-friendly twist on a classic human indulgence. Crafting these tail-wagging delights is an expression of love and an exploration into the art of canine nutrition and the joyous process of creating a midday treat that mirrors the flavors and textures our dogs find irresistible. This section embarks on a flavorful journey, unraveling the nutritional benefits, ingredient considerations, and the joy of preparing DIY doggy burgers for a midday treat. This canine culinary adventure celebrates the bond between humans and their four-legged companions.

The commitment to providing our canine friends with wholesome and nutritious treats is at the heart of DIY doggy burgers. The choice of ingredients becomes paramount in ensuring that the burgers not only tantalize the taste buds but also contribute to the overall well-being of our dogs. Whether beef, turkey, or chicken, lean ground meat serves as the primary protein source, offering essential amino acids crucial for muscle development and maintenance. Including vegetables, such as carrots, peas, or sweet potatoes, adds a burst of vitamins, minerals, and dietary fiber—a nod to the importance of a balanced and varied diet for our canine friends.

Nutritional balance in DIY doggy burgers extends beyond macronutrients, encompassing a spectrum of micronutrients supporting canine health. Eggs, a common binding ingredient in canine-friendly recipes, provide a source of high-quality protein and essential fatty acids. Adding whole grains, like oats or brown rice, introduces complex carbohydrates that contribute to sustained energy levels. Adding ingredients like flaxseed or chia seeds enhances the omega-3 fatty acid content, promoting skin and coat health. The careful balance of these components ensures that DIY doggy burgers are not just a tasty treat but a nutritionally sound addition to a dog's diet.

The culinary canvas for DIY doggy burgers invites creativity and customization, allowing pet owners to tailor the treats to their dogs' unique preferences and dietary needs. Vegetables can be finely grated or pureed for picky eaters, while those with food sensitivities might benefit from grain-free alternatives. The size and shape of the burgers can be adjusted to accommodate dogs of different breeds and sizes, ensuring that each furry friend receives a portion that suits their needs. This adaptability underscores the personalized and caring nature of creating DIY doggy burgers.

Preparing DIY doggy burgers transforms mealtime into a shared culinary adventure between pet owners and their dogs. The aromatic scent of cooking meat and the sizzle of ingredients on the stovetop create an atmosphere of anticipation and excitement. Shaping and forming the burgers becomes a hands-on experience that fosters a sense of connection and engagement. As the burgers cook, the air is filled with the irresistible fragrance that signals the imminent delight awaiting our canine companions. This sensory journey enhances the joy of treating our dogs to a homemade culinary creation.

In the landscape of canine nutrition, the transparency and control afforded by DIY doggy burgers address the concerns surrounding commercial dog treats. Many store-bought treats contain additives, preservatives, and potential allergens that may not align with a dog's dietary needs. Crafting treats at home allows pet owners to be fully aware of the ingredients used, avoiding fillers, artificial colors, and unnecessary additives. The choice of high-quality, whole-food ingredients ensures that each DIY doggy burger is a pure and wholesome indulgence free from hidden ingredients that might compromise a dog's well-being.

The nutritional benefits of DIY doggy burgers extend beyond the immediate joy of a tasty treat to impact broader aspects of canine health. Including fresh ingredients contributes to overall digestive well-being, as the dietary fiber from vegetables and whole grains promotes healthy digestion and regular bowel movements. The omega-3 fatty acids from ingredients like flaxseed or fish oil support skin health and coat shine, addressing common concerns such as dry skin or dull fur. The mindful selection of ingredients also allows pet owners to tailor the burgers to address specific dietary needs, whether weight management, food sensitivities, or preferences.

Offering DIY doggy burgers becomes a gesture of love and care—a shared moment that strengthens the bond between pet owners and their dogs. The excitement and enthusiasm dogs exhibit as they receive a homemade treat underscore the joy derived from the shared experience. Treating our dogs to a culinary creation made with love and consideration transcends the realm of nutrition to reflect the deep connection and mutual affection between humans and their four-legged companions.

In the landscape of canine health, the DIY approach to doggy burgers allows pet owners to cater to the specific needs of individual dogs. For example, older dogs may benefit from including joint-friendly ingredients like turmeric or glucosamine. Puppies, on the other hand, may require a higher protein content to support growth and development. The adaptability of DIY doggy burgers accommodates these diverse needs, providing a versatile and customizable treat that evolves with the changing requirements of a dog's life stages.

The rising popularity of DIY doggy burgers aligns with the broader movement towards conscious and mindful pet ownership. Pet owners increasingly seek to extend their commitment to health and well-being to their canine companions. Social media platforms showcase many images and videos featuring proud pet owners presenting their homemade canine creations, inspiring a global community to embrace the joy of crafting nutritious and delicious treats for their dogs.

The hashtag #DIYDogTreats has become a hub for sharing recipes, tips, and heartwarming moments of canine culinary enjoyment.

In conclusion, the joy and nutritional benefits of crafting DIY doggy burgers for a midday treat epitomize the intersection of love, nutrition, and culinary creativity in pet care. These canine-friendly burgers are more than a delectable indulgence; they represent a thoughtful and hands-on approach to canine nutrition, fostering a bond of care and connection between pet owners and their dogs. As the popularity of DIY doggy burgers continues to grow, it stands as a testament to the evolving landscape of pet care. This movement celebrates the joy of treating our dogs to a delicious culinary experience.

# CHAPTER VI

# Delicious Dinner Delights

## Gourmet Meatloaf for Picky Eaters

In comfort food, meatloaf is a classic that resonates with memories of home-cooked meals and hearty indulgence. However, elevating this timeless dish to gourmet status introduces a culinary challenge that demands finesse, creativity, and a keen understanding of flavors. This section delves into the artistry of crafting gourmet meatloaf, with a particular focus on catering to the discerning palates of picky eaters. From ingredient considerations to cooking techniques, the journey of transforming a humble meatloaf into a gourmet delight becomes a celebration of culinary finesse and a testament to the power of gastronomic creativity in satisfying even the most selective taste buds.

At the heart of crafting gourmet meatloaf for picky eaters lies the meticulous selection of high-quality ingredients that contribute to both flavor complexity and nutritional value. While traditional meatloaf recipes often rely on a mixture of ground beef and pork, gourmet variations may introduce exotic meats such as lamb, veal, or even a blend of meats to elevate the dish's richness and depth of flavor. The choice of breadcrumbs, whether sourced from artisanal bread or a mix of grains, adds texture and character. Gourmet meatloaf often incorporates a medley of finely chopped vegetables, from caramelized onions to sautéed mushrooms, to infuse additional layers of flavor and moisture.

The key to success in crafting gourmet meatloaf for picky eaters lies in striking a delicate balance between sophistication and familiarity. While the goal is to introduce elevated flavors and textures, it is equally important to anchor the dish in elements that resonate with the preferences of picky eaters. Gourmet meatloaf might feature a delectable glaze made from balsamic reduction or a blend of exotic spices, offering a departure from the traditional ketchup-based topping. However, the inclusion of familiar herbs, such as thyme or rosemary, ensures a bridge between the gourmet twist and the comfort of the familiar.

Texture plays a crucial role in the appeal of gourmet meatloaf, especially when catering to picky eaters with specific textural preferences. The incorporation of ingredients like finely chopped nuts or seeds adds a delightful crunch, while the use of ingredients such as quinoa or farro introduces a chewy element that contrasts with the tender meat. These textural nuances not only contribute to the overall sensory experience but also provide picky eaters with a diverse range of mouthfeel that can captivate their taste buds and overcome resistance to more conventional meatloaf textures.

Cooking techniques in the realm of gourmet meatloaf elevate the dish from a humble baked offering to a culinary masterpiece. While traditional meatloaf is often baked in a loaf pan, gourmet variations may be shaped into elegant rolls or individual servings that enhance presentation and allow for controlled portioning. The incorporation of slow-cooking methods, such as braising or sous-vide cooking, imparts a level of tenderness and flavor infusion that transcends the conventional baking approach. The choice of cooking method becomes a crucial aspect of crafting gourmet meatloaf that appeals to discerning palates.

Sauces and accompaniments become a playground for gourmet creativity when crafting meatloaf for picky eaters. A drizzle of truffle-infused gravy, a velvety mushroom cream sauce, or a tangy fruit compote can elevate the entire dining experience. These gourmet accompaniments not only add layers of flavor but also serve as a means of customization, allowing picky eaters to choose elements that align with their preferences. The artful presentation of the sauce becomes a visual cue that signals the gourmet nature of the dish, enticing picky eaters to explore beyond their culinary comfort zones.

In the landscape of dietary considerations, the adaptability of gourmet meatloaf becomes a valuable asset when catering to picky eaters with specific nutritional needs. For those seeking a lighter option, lean meats or plant-based alternatives can be incorporated without compromising on flavor. Gluten-free breadcrumbs or alternative binders accommodate individuals with dietary restrictions, offering a gourmet meatloaf experience that is inclusive and mindful of diverse nutritional requirements. The customization possibilities ensure that gourmet meatloaf can align with a wide range of dietary preferences and restrictions.

The appeal of gourmet meatloaf for picky eaters extends beyond the confines of home kitchens to find resonance in the culinary landscape of restaurants and gourmet food establishments. As the demand for elevated comfort food experiences grows, chefs are increasingly turning their attention to reinventing classic dishes, including meatloaf, to cater to the discerning tastes of a diverse clientele. Gourmet meatloaf may find its place on upscale menus, accompanied by curated sides and thoughtful wine pairings, transforming a humble dish into a culinary delight fit for the most sophisticated palates.

The culinary experience of savoring gourmet meatloaf becomes a journey of discovery for picky eaters, inviting them to explore the nuances of flavors, textures, and presentations that transcend the ordinary. The act of transforming a familiar dish into a gourmet creation not only challenges palates but also engages picky eaters in a sensory adventure that broadens their culinary horizons. The approach becomes less about coaxing picky eaters into accepting new flavors and more about creating an enticing and immersive dining experience that naturally draws them into the world of gourmet comfort food.

The rising trend of gourmet comfort food, including gourmet meatloaf, is evident in the vast array of online platforms dedicated to culinary exploration and recipe sharing. Food blogs, cooking websites, and social media platforms are adorned with images and recipes showcasing the artful transformation of classic dishes into gourmet masterpieces. The hashtag #GourmetMeatloaf has become a rallying point for chefs, home cooks, and food enthusiasts to share their inventive takes on this beloved comfort food, inspiring a global community to embark on their own gourmet culinary adventures.

In conclusion, the art of crafting gourmet meatloaf for picky eaters is a celebration of culinary finesse, creativity, and the ability to elevate a classic dish to new heights. From meticulous ingredient selection to innovative cooking techniques, the journey of transforming meatloaf becomes an exploration into the diverse world of flavors and textures. Gourmet meatloaf, presented with flair and accompanied by complementary sauces, offers picky eaters an opportunity to engage with familiar ingredients in an entirely new light. As the culinary landscape continues to evolve, gourmet meatloaf stands as a testament to the power of culinary creativity in transforming the ordinary into the extraordinary.

## Fishy Feast with Omega-3 Rich Ingredients

In the realm of culinary delights, the integration of omega-3 rich ingredients into a fishy feast not only elevates the dining experience but also offers a plethora of health benefits that resonate with the principles of mindful eating. Omega-3 fatty acids, found abundantly in fatty fish, seeds, and certain oils, are renowned for their cardiovascular benefits, cognitive support, and anti-inflammatory properties. This section embarks on a flavorful journey into the world of fishy feasts enriched with omega-3, exploring the nutritional significance, diverse culinary expressions, and the sheer pleasure derived from crafting a meal that nourishes both the body and the soul.

At the heart of a fishy feast with omega-3 rich ingredients lies a profound appreciation for the nutritional bounty offered by the ocean. Fatty fish, such as salmon, mackerel, and trout, take center stage, serving as the primary sources of eicosapentaenoic acid (EPA) and docosahexaenoic acid (DHA)—two essential forms of omega-3 fatty acids.

These fatty acids are recognized for their role in supporting heart health, reducing inflammation, and contributing to cognitive function. The inclusion of other omega-3 rich ingredients, such as chia seeds, flaxseeds, and walnuts, further enhances the nutritional diversity of the fishy feast, creating a symphony of flavors and health benefits.

The nutritional density of a fishy feast enriched with omega-3 extends beyond the primary fatty acids to encompass a spectrum of vitamins, minerals, and antioxidants. Fatty fish, in addition to providing omega-3, offer an excellent source of high-quality protein, B vitamins, and minerals such as selenium and iodine. The incorporation of omega-3 rich seeds and nuts introduces dietary fiber, additional protein, and an array of micronutrients, contributing to the overall nutritional balance of the feast. Vegetables, whether roasted, sautéed, or served raw, infuse the meal with vitamins, minerals, and phytonutrients that support immune function and cellular health.

Culinary creativity takes center stage in the preparation of a fishy feast with omega-3 rich ingredients, offering a diverse range of techniques and flavor profiles. The art of grilling or baking fatty fish enhances their natural richness while preserving the delicate texture. A tangy and herb-infused marinade or a zesty citrus glaze can add layers of flavor that complement the inherent taste of the fish. Omega-3 rich seeds, when toasted, impart a nutty crunch to salads or sides, while a drizzle of flaxseed oil or a sprinkle of chia seeds elevates the nutritional profile of dressings and sauces. The versatility of omega-3 rich ingredients becomes a canvas for culinary expression, allowing chefs and home cooks alike to explore a multitude of flavors and textures.

In the global tapestry of culinary traditions, a fishy feast with omega-3 rich ingredients finds expression in diverse and culturally distinct ways. The Japanese celebration of sashimi showcases the pristine quality of raw fish, emphasizing its delicate flavor and texture. Mediterranean cuisines often feature grilled fish seasoned with herbs, olive oil, and lemon, exemplifying the harmonious integration of omega-3 rich ingredients into regional dishes. Scandinavian cultures celebrate the richness of fatty fish through traditional dishes like gravlax, where salmon is cured with a blend of sugar, salt, and dill. Each cultural interpretation of a fishy feast with omega-3 reflects the unique flavors and culinary techniques that have evolved to showcase the nutritional and gastronomic virtues of the ocean's bounty.

The sensory delight derived from a fishy feast with

omega-3 rich ingredients transcends the plate to engage sight, smell, and taste. The vibrant hues of grilled salmon, the glossy sheen of omega-3 rich oils, and the colorful medley of vegetables create a visually appealing tableau that entices the diner. The aroma of grilled fish, infused with herbs and citrus, wafts through the air, creating an olfactory prelude to the feast. As the first bite is savored, the interplay of textures—from the flaky fish to the crunchy seeds and tender vegetables—enhances the overall dining experience, creating a symphony of flavors that captivates the palate.

The health benefits associated with omega-3 fatty acids

contribute to the allure of a fishy feast, making it not just a delicious indulgence but a strategic choice for overall well-being. The cardioprotective effects of omega-3, including the reduction of triglycerides, blood pressure, and inflammation, position a fishy feast as a heart-healthy option. The cognitive benefits, such as improved brain function and a potential protective role against cognitive decline, underscore the importance of omega-3 in supporting mental well-being. The anti-inflammatory properties of omega-3 further contribute to a holistic approach to health, addressing conditions ranging from arthritis to skin health.

In the landscape of contemporary dietary preferences, a fishy feast with omega-3 rich ingredients aligns with the principles of a balanced and health-conscious diet. The emphasis on high-quality proteins, essential fatty acids, and nutrient-dense vegetables resonates with those seeking a nutrient-rich meal that supports overall health. The inclusion of omega-3 rich ingredients accommodates dietary preferences and restrictions, offering options for those following pescatarian, Mediterranean, or anti-inflammatory diets. The adaptability of a fishy feast makes it a versatile and accessible choice for individuals navigating diverse nutritional needs.

The popularity of a fishy feast with omega-3 rich ingredients extends beyond home kitchens to find resonance in restaurants, seafood markets, and health-focused eateries. Menus increasingly highlight the nutritional benefits of omega-3 and showcase dishes that celebrate the diverse flavors of fatty fish and other omega-3 rich ingredients. The culinary movement is amplified on social media platforms, where hashtags such as #Omega3Feast or #HealthySeafood celebrate the culinary creativity and nutritional wisdom associated with integrating omega-3 into a fishy feast.

In conclusion, the crafting of a fishy feast with omega-3 rich ingredients is a celebration of both culinary artistry and nutritional wisdom. The symphony of flavors, textures, and cultural expressions that converge in this feast reflects the diverse ways in which omega-3 can be integrated into a gastronomic masterpiece. Beyond the palate, the health benefits associated with omega-3 underscore the holistic approach to well-being that a fishy feast offers. Whether enjoyed in the comforts of home, at a seafood restaurant, or as part of a cultural celebration, a fishy feast with omega-3 rich ingredients stands as a testament to the enduring appeal of culinary indulgence that nourishes the body and delights the senses.

## Vegetable-Packed Dinner Bowls

In the ever-evolving landscape of culinary trends, vegetable-packed dinner bowls have emerged as a versatile and nourishing delight that celebrates the vibrant diversity of plant-based ingredients. These bowls, adorned with a colorful array of vegetables, whole grains, proteins, and flavorful sauces, offer a visual and gastronomic feast that resonates with the principles of balanced nutrition and culinary creativity. This section embarks on a flavorful exploration into the world of vegetable-packed dinner bowls, unraveling their nutritional significance, culinary diversity, and the sheer joy they bring to the table—a celebration of harmony, flavor, and nourishment in every delightful bite.

At the core of the appeal of vegetable-packed dinner bowls is the commitment to harnessing the nutritional power of a variety of plant-based ingredients. The foundation of these bowls often rests on a base of whole grains, such as quinoa, brown rice, or farro, providing complex carbohydrates that serve as a sustained source of energy. The inclusion of a colorful medley of vegetables—from leafy greens and cruciferous varieties to vibrant bell peppers, tomatoes, and avocados—infuses the bowls with a diverse array of vitamins, minerals, and antioxidants. Proteins, whether sourced from legumes, tofu, tempeh, or lean animal proteins, contribute to the satiety and provide essential amino acids crucial for muscle development and overall well-being.

Nutritional balance takes center stage in vegetable-packed dinner bowls, aligning with the principles of mindful eating and health-conscious choices. The bowls effortlessly integrate macronutrients—carbohydrates, proteins, and fats—while ensuring a rich supply of micronutrients crucial for supporting immune function, promoting skin health, and contributing to overall vitality. The inclusion of healthy fats, derived from sources like avocados, nuts, or olive oil, completes the nutritional ensemble, supporting cognitive function and enhancing the absorption of fat-soluble vitamins.

Culinary creativity flourishes in the construction of vegetable-packed dinner bowls, offering a canvas for the artful assembly of flavors, textures, and visual appeal. The process begins with the choice of grains, where the selection of quinoa or brown rice sets the tone for the bowl. Proteins, whether grilled, roasted, or sautéed, lend a savory depth to the ensemble. The addition of a diverse array of vegetables—raw, roasted, or pickled—provides a burst of freshness, while toppings like seeds, nuts, or cheese contribute contrasting textures and flavors. Sauces and dressings, from tahini-based blends to zesty vinaigrettes, tie the components together, elevating the entire bowl into a delectable and cohesive culinary creation.

The global culinary tapestry is vividly represented in the myriad variations of vegetable-packed dinner bowls that draw inspiration from diverse culinary traditions. The Buddha Bowl, originating from the principles of Buddhist cuisine, emphasizes balance and simplicity with a harmonious mix of grains, vegetables, proteins, and a flavorful sauce. The Poke Bowl, inspired by Hawaiian cuisine, showcases raw fish, seaweed, and a variety of vegetables atop a base of rice or greens, offering a refreshing and vibrant experience. The Mediterranean Bowl, featuring ingredients like falafel, olives, and hummus, pays homage to the flavors of the Mediterranean region. These bowls become vessels for cultural expression, embodying the essence of regional ingredients, preparation techniques, and culinary aesthetics.

The sensory delight derived from vegetable-packed dinner bowls engages not only the taste buds but also sight, smell, and texture. The vibrant colors of fresh vegetables, the aromatic allure of roasted or grilled proteins, and the contrasting textures of crunchy nuts or creamy avocados create a visual and olfactory spectacle that heightens the overall dining experience. The act of assembling and enjoying the bowl becomes a ritual that fosters a mindful connection with the food, inviting individuals to appreciate the diversity of flavors and the nutritional bounty within each carefully curated bite.

In the landscape of dietary wellness, vegetable-packed dinner bowls emerge as a strategic tool for achieving and maintaining nutritional equilibrium. The inclusion of a variety of vegetables provides a spectrum of vitamins, minerals, and phytonutrients that support overall health and well-being. The adaptability of the bowls allows for customization based on individual dietary preferences and restrictions, making them accessible and inclusive for individuals following vegetarian, vegan, gluten-free, or other specific diets. The bowls also align with dietary guidelines promoting increased vegetable intake, fiber consumption, and a reduction in processed foods.

The convenience and efficiency of vegetable-packed dinner bowls align with the demands of modern lifestyles, offering a solution for individuals seeking wholesome and time-efficient meal options. The prep-ahead nature of many components—such as batch-cooked grains, roasted vegetables, and homemade sauces—streamlines the assembly process, making dinner bowls an accessible choice for those with busy schedules. The portability of dinner bowls also caters to individuals on the go, allowing them to enjoy a nutritious and satisfying meal without compromising on flavor or nutritional quality.

The culinary phenomenon of vegetable-packed dinner bowls is not confined to home kitchens; it has permeated restaurant menus, cafes, and food establishments worldwide. The popularity of customizable bowl concepts, where patrons can select their preferred grains, proteins, vegetables, and toppings, reflects the widespread appeal of this culinary trend. The social media landscape further amplifies the trend, with Instagram feeds adorned with visually stunning images of vibrant dinner bowls that serve as both culinary inspiration and a celebration of wholesome, balanced eating.

The conscious effort to reduce environmental impact finds resonance in the ethos of vegetable-packed dinner bowls, where plant-based ingredients take center stage. The bowls offer a sustainable and eco-friendly dining option that aligns with the principles of reducing meat consumption and choosing ingredients with a lower carbon footprint. The focus on seasonal, locally sourced produce contributes to a more sustainable food system, fostering a connection between individuals and the origins of their food.

In conclusion, the rise of vegetable-packed dinner bowls symbolizes a culinary movement that harmonizes nutritional principles with diverse flavors, textures, and cultural influences. These bowls encapsulate the essence of modern dietary preferences, emphasizing balance, mindfulness, and culinary enjoyment. Whether savored at home, prepared with love in a family kitchen, or enjoyed at a bustling restaurant, the appeal of vegetable-packed dinner bowls lies in their ability to transcend the boundaries of tradition, offering a dynamic and flavorful canvas that adapts to the evolving palate and nutritional goals of individuals worldwide.

# CHAPTER VII

# Tasty Treats and Snacks

## Crunchy Peanut Butter Biscuits

In baked delights, few treats can rival peanut butter biscuits' comforting and indulgent allure. Among the diverse peanut butter creations, crunchy peanut butter biscuits are a delightful symphony of flavor and texture. These biscuits, adorned with the unmistakable crunch of roasted peanuts and the rich, nutty notes of peanut butter, offer a culinary experience that transcends the ordinary. This section delves into the artistry of crafting crunchy peanut butter biscuits, exploring the history, ingredients, baking techniques, and the sheer joy they bring to palates —a celebration of the harmonious marriage of peanuts and biscuits that has captivated taste buds around the world.

The story of crunchy peanut butter biscuits unfolds

against the backdrop of a rich history that intertwines biscuit-making traditions and the timeless appeal of peanut butter. Peanut butter, a staple in many households, traces its roots back to the Aztecs and Incas, who ground roasted peanuts into a paste. However, in the early 20th century, peanut butter gained widespread popularity in the United States, and its integration into various culinary creations, including biscuits, became a testament to the versatility of this beloved spread. Including crunchy peanut butter—a variation that retains chopped peanuts for added texture—introduced a delightful twist to the classic peanut butter biscuit, offering a sensory adventure encompassing smooth creaminess and satisfying crunch.

Crafting crunchy peanut butter biscuits begins with the meticulous selection of high-quality ingredients that define the flavor profile and texture of the final product. The choice of peanut butter becomes a pivotal decision, with some bakers opting for commercially available varieties. In contrast, others create homemade peanut butter for a truly bespoke experience. Including roasted peanuts, finely chopped or coarsely ground, enhances the crunch factor, infusing the biscuits with a distinctive texture that elevates them beyond the standard peanut butter cookie. High-quality flour, butter, and sugar complement the peanut goodness, creating a harmonious blend of flavors that characterize these biscuits.

The baking process becomes a delicate dance of precision and creativity when crafting crunchy peanut butter biscuits. Exact measures and meticulous temperature control are vital to the ideal balance between a golden outside and a chewy, soft inside. Incorporating leavening agents, such as baking soda or baking powder, imparts a lightness to the biscuits, ensuring they achieve the ideal rise during baking. Shaping the biscuits—through traditional rolling and cutting or the more modern drop-cookie method—becomes a hands-on expression of the baker's skill and personal touch. As the biscuits emerge from the oven, the enticing aroma of roasted peanuts and freshly baked goodness fills the kitchen, signaling the imminent delight awaiting those fortunate enough to indulge.

The symphony of flavors in crunchy peanut butter biscuits extends beyond the peanuts, encompassing a delicate interplay of sweet and savory notes. The inclusion of sugars—whether white or brown—balances the inherent nuttiness of the peanuts, creating a nuanced sweetness that complements the richness of the peanut butter. A pinch of salt, often added to the dough, heightens the savory undertones, accentuating the complexity of flavors. Some recipes may introduce additional elements, such as vanilla extract or a hint of cinnamon, to enhance the overall taste profile. The result is a biscuit tantalizing the taste buds with a sophisticated blend of sweet, salty, and nutty nuances.

Crunchy peanut butter biscuits hold a special place in the hearts of those who appreciate the sensory pleasure of contrasting textures. The satisfying crunch of roasted peanuts, dispersed throughout the tender crumb of the biscuit, creates a dynamic mouthfeel that elevates the overall experience. Biting into a biscuit, with its exterior delicately yielding to the teeth before revealing the crunchy interior, becomes a sensory delight that lingers in the memory. This textural symphony sets crunchy peanut butter biscuits apart, inviting enthusiasts to savor the moment and appreciate the craftsmanship of creating such a delectable treat.

The universal appeal of crunchy peanut butter biscuits is evident in their ability to transcend cultural boundaries and find a place on tables worldwide. While peanut butter has become a global culinary phenomenon, incorporating this beloved spread into biscuits has resulted in a confluence of flavors that resonates with people from diverse backgrounds. Whether enjoyed with a cup of tea in the United Kingdom, as a snack in the United States, or as part of a festive celebration in Asia, crunchy peanut butter biscuits have become a symbol of the shared pleasure derived from simple yet masterfully crafted baked goods.

Sharing crunchy peanut butter biscuits extends beyond the physical exchange of treats; it becomes a gesture of warmth, hospitality, and connection. Bakers often enjoy preparing batches of these biscuits to share with friends, family, or colleagues. With its irresistible combination of crunch and creaminess, the humble biscuit becomes a token of affection that transcends language and cultural differences. The communal experience of indulging in crunchy peanut butter biscuits fosters a sense of togetherness and shared enjoyment, creating lasting memories around the simple pleasure of a well-crafted treat.

In the realm of dietary considerations, crunchy peanut butter biscuits offer a versatile option that accommodates a variety of preferences and restrictions. The essential ingredients—peanut butter, flour, sugar, and peanuts— form a foundation that can be adapted to suit different dietary needs. Gluten-free flours can be substituted for traditional flour to create a gluten-free version, while alternative sweeteners reduce refined sugars. Including whole peanuts introduces an additional protein and healthy fat source, aligning these biscuits with a more mindful approach to snacking and dessert choices.

The popularity of crunchy peanut butter biscuits is amplified in the digital age, where social media platforms showcase many images and recipes that celebrate the artistry of biscuit-making. Hashtags such as #PeanutButterBiscuits and #CrunchyCookies are virtual hubs for enthusiasts to share their baking adventures, exchange tips, and revel in creating and savoring these beloved treats. The global online community dedicated to crunchy peanut butter biscuits underscores the enduring charm of this classic baked good, inviting individuals from all walks of life to join the conversation and contribute to the collective love for these delightful creations.

In conclusion, crafting crunchy peanut butter biscuits is a celebration of flavor, texture, and the timeless appeal of a well-executed baked treat. From the humble origins of peanut butter to the nuanced artistry of biscuit-making, these biscuits embody a harmonious fusion of ingredients that has captivated taste buds for generations. Whether enjoyed as a comforting indulgence with a cup of tea or shared as a gesture of hospitality, crunchy peanut butter biscuits stand as a testament to the enduring pleasure derived from the symphony of peanuts, butter, and crunch. This culinary masterpiece continues to delight and unite enthusiasts around the world.

# Frozen Yogurt Pops for Summer

Finding excellent snacks to beat the summer heat becomes a gastronomic adventure as the temperature increases and the sun beams down on the sky. In this pursuit of fantastic delights, frozen yogurt pops emerge as a delightful and health-conscious option that marries the creamy indulgence of frozen yogurt with the convenience of a handheld treat. This section explores the art of crafting frozen yogurt pops for summer—a celebration of flavor, creativity, and the sheer joy of indulging in a cool, palate-pleasing sensation that encapsulates the essence of the sun-soaked season.

The concept of frozen yogurt, a versatile and lighter alternative to traditional ice cream, gained popularity in the latter half of the 20th century and has since become a beloved frozen dessert. Frozen yogurt pops, an extension of this trend, offer a playful twist by transforming the creamy goodness into a convenient and portable form. The appeal of frozen yogurt lies in its tangy profile, lower fat content, and the potential for incorporating a variety of flavors, making it an ideal canvas for creating a diverse array of frozen treats.

Crafting the perfect frozen yogurt pop begins with selecting high-quality ingredients that form the foundation of the frozen delight. Prized for its thick and creamy texture, Greek yogurt often takes center stage, providing a rich base that lends itself well to freezing. The choice of sweeteners, whether natural options like honey agave nectar or more traditional sugars, allows for customization based on taste preferences. Fresh fruits, purees, or extracts become the flavor ambassadors, infusing the pops with a burst of fruity goodness. Adding extras like nuts, chocolate chips, or granola introduces delightful textural elements that surprise and delight with every bite.

Crafting frozen yogurt pops is a delightful journey of blending, pouring, and freezing—a symphony of flavors and textures coming together to create an icy masterpiece. The yogurt mixture, enriched with the chosen flavors and additions, is carefully poured into molds that come in an array of shapes and sizes, from classic popsicle molds to whimsical designs that add an element of fun to the frozen treat experience. Inserting sticks transforms the creamy concoction into a handheld delight, ready to be frozen to perfection.

As the frozen yogurt pops set in the freezer, the anticipation builds, and the transformation from liquid to solid becomes a process of culinary alchemy. The low temperatures gradually crystallize the mixture, creating a smooth yet icy texture that is the hallmark of a well-crafted frozen yogurt pop. The frozen treats are a canvas for creativity, allowing for layers, swirls, or even artistic patterns that enhance the visual appeal, making them as pleasing to the eyes as they are to the palate.

The flavor possibilities are endless regarding frozen yogurt pops, offering a spectrum that caters to a wide range of taste preferences. From classic combinations like strawberry-banana or blueberry-vanilla to more adventurous pairings like mango-coconut or raspberry-lime, the frozen yogurt pop becomes a playground for flavor experimentation. Adding herbs, such as mint or basil, introduces a refreshing herbal note, while spices like cinnamon or cardamom can add a warm and exotic touch. The beauty of crafting frozen yogurt pops lies in the ability to tailor them to suit individual tastes, creating a personalized frozen indulgence that satisfies the summer sweet tooth.

The allure of frozen yogurt pops extends beyond flavor to encompass the nutritional appeal of these frozen delights. Greek yogurt, a staple in many recipes, contributes not only to the creamy texture but also adds a protein boost, making the frozen treats a satisfying and wholesome snack. Incorporating fresh fruits introduces a medley of vitamins, minerals, and antioxidants, elevating the nutritional profile of the pops. The option to control the sweetness level and choose healthier sweeteners aligns with the growing trend of mindful and health-conscious eating, allowing individuals to indulge without compromising nutritional values.

The enjoyment of frozen yogurt pops becomes a multisensory experience as the summer sun bathes the surroundings in warmth. The act of unwrapping a frozen yogurt pop is a moment of anticipation, and the first lick or bite introduces a refreshing chill that provides instant relief from the heat. The creaminess of the yogurt mingles with the burst of fruity flavors creates a harmonious dance in the taste buds. The smooth and icy texture adds an element of surprise and excitement, making each bite or lick a journey of sensory delight.

The cultural ubiquity of frozen treats during the summer months is evident across the globe, with various regions putting their spin on frozen yogurt pops. In Mediterranean countries, frozen yogurt pops may feature the rich flavor of strained yogurt, complemented by honey and chopped nuts. In tropical regions, coconut milk and exotic fruits take center stage, offering a taste of the tropics in a frozen form. In East Asia, inventive flavors like matcha green tea or lychee may grace frozen yogurt pops, showcasing the culinary diversity that summer inspires worldwide.

The social aspect of enjoying frozen yogurt pops further enhances their appeal, transforming the frozen treat into a shared experience. Whether enjoyed at family gatherings, picnics, or by the poolside, offering and accepting a frozen yogurt pop becomes a gesture of camaraderie and shared enjoyment. The communal aspect extends to creating frozen yogurt pops at home, where families or friends can gather to experiment with flavors, pour the mixture into molds, and eagerly wait for the firm results—an activity that brings joy and togetherness to the summer season.

In dietary inclusivity, frozen yogurt is a versatile treat that accommodates various nutritional preferences and restrictions. The inherent flexibility of the recipe allows for the incorporation of dairy-free yogurt alternatives, making the pops accessible to those with lactose intolerance or following a plant-based diet. Using alternative sweeteners caters to individuals seeking lower sugar options or adhering to specific dietary guidelines. The customization possibilities ensure that frozen yogurt pops can align with diverse nutritional needs, making them an inclusive and enjoyable treat for a broad audience.

The popularity of frozen yogurt pops is amplified in contemporary times by the omnipresence of social media, where images and recipes of these frozen delights take center stage. Hashtags like #FrozenYogurtPops or #SummerTreats become digital hubs for enthusiasts to share frozen yogurt pop creations, exchange flavor ideas, and showcase vibrant and visually appealing results. The online community dedicated to frozen yogurt pops is an inspiration source, inviting individuals to embark on their own frozen treat adventures and contribute to the collective celebration of summer indulgence.

In conclusion, crafting frozen yogurt pops for summer is a celebration of flavor, creativity, and the simple joys of indulging in a cool, refreshing treat. From the creamy base of Greek yogurt to the vibrant burst of fresh fruits and the endless flavor possibilities, these frozen delights encapsulate the essence of summer in every bite. Whether enjoyed solo on a hot afternoon or shared with loved ones at a gathering, frozen yogurt pops are a testament to the timeless pleasure derived from the marriage of sweet, tangy, and icy—a delightful symphony that transforms the summer heat into a blissful and relaxed celebration.

## Nutritious Fruit Bites for Training

In the pursuit of optimal performance and sustained energy during training, the significance of nutrition becomes a cornerstone for athletes and fitness enthusiasts alike. Among the myriad options available, nutritious fruit bites emerge as a flavorful and wholesome choice that not only satiates hunger but also provides essential nutrients to support the demands of physical activity. This section delves into the art of crafting nutritious fruit bites for training—an exploration of ingredients, nutritional benefits, and the culinary creativity that transforms simple fruits into convenient and energizing fuel for peak performance.

The foundation of nutritious fruit bites lies in selecting high-quality ingredients that balance carbohydrates, natural sugars, vitamins, and minerals. Dried fruits, such as dates, figs, apricots, or raisins, become the base, providing a concentrated energy source from natural sugars, fiber, antioxidants, and essential micronutrients. Including nuts, seeds, or nut butter introduces healthy fats and proteins, creating a satiating blend that supports sustained energy release. Adding whole grains, such as oats or quinoa, contributes complex carbohydrates and additional fiber, enhancing the nutritional density of these bites.

The crafting process involves a symphony of flavors and textures, aiming to achieve a delicious and nutrient-dense composition. Dried fruits, chosen for their sweetness and chewiness, are often combined with nuts or seeds to introduce a crunch and nuttiness that complements the natural sugars. The use of nut butter not only binds the ingredients together but also imparts a creamy texture and enhances the overall flavor profile. Whole grains, when incorporated, add a hearty texture and a subtle nuttiness, contributing to the satisfying nature of these bites. The options for flavor enhancement are vast, including ingredients like cocoa powder, vanilla extract, or spices, allowing for customization based on individual taste preferences.

Nutritious fruit bites cater to the nutritional requirements of athletes by providing a well-rounded combination of macronutrients and micronutrients. Carbohydrates, derived from the natural sugars in dried fruits and whole grains, are the primary energy source, replenishing glycogen stores and fueling muscles during exercise. Proteins from nuts, seeds, or nut butter contribute to muscle repair and maintenance, supporting recovery after strenuous physical activity. Healthy fats in nuts and seeds play a crucial role in hormone production, joint health, and the absorption of fat-soluble vitamins. The various ingredients' abundance of vitamins, minerals, and antioxidants further supports overall health and immune function, helping athletes withstand the rigors of training.

The convenience of nutritious fruit bites extends beyond their nutritional prowess, making them an ideal snack for on-the-go fueling during training sessions. The bite-sized nature of these treats ensures portability, allowing athletes to carry them easily in gym bags, pockets, or hydration belts. The absence of perishable ingredients makes them a durable and shelf-stable option, suitable for extended training sessions or outdoor activities where refrigeration may not be readily available. The quick energy release from the natural sugars in dried fruits provides an immediate fuel source, making these bites an efficient choice for maintaining energy levels during workouts.

The sensory pleasure derived from nutritious fruit bites transcends their functional benefits, engaging taste buds with a symphony of flavors. The sweetness of dried fruits, balanced by the nuttiness of seeds or nuts and the creaminess of nut butter, creates a harmonious blend that satisfies sweet cravings without relying on refined sugars. The texture, whether chewy from dried fruits or crunchy from nuts and seeds, adds a delightful element to the eating experience. Including flavor enhancers like cocoa or spices introduces depth and complexity, ensuring each bite is a sensory delight that resonates with the palate.

Regarding dietary preferences and restrictions, nutritious fruit bites accommodate various eating patterns, including vegetarian, vegan, gluten-free, and nut-free diets. The flexibility in ingredient choices allows for customization based on individual dietary needs, making these bites accessible to a diverse range of athletes. The absence of common allergens and the reliance on whole, minimally processed ingredients align with the principles of clean eating, offering a snack option that supports both performance and overall well-being.

The crafting of nutritious fruit bites is not limited to home kitchens; it has found resonance in the commercial market, where energy bars, bites, and similar products cater to the demands of fitness enthusiasts. Brands often highlight their products' natural and wholesome ingredients, appealing to consumers seeking convenient and nutritious pre- and post-workout snacks. The popularity of these products is amplified by marketing campaigns that emphasize their role in supporting athletic performance, muscle recovery, and overall health. As a result, nutritious fruit bites have become a staple in the sports nutrition landscape, offering a flavorful and functional choice for those committed to an active lifestyle.

The cultural and culinary diversity of nutritious fruit bites is evident in the variations that draw inspiration from global cuisines. Mediterranean-inspired bites may feature dried apricots, figs, and pistachios, evoking the region's flavors. Tropical variations include dried pineapple, coconut, and macadamia nuts for a taste of the islands. Asian-infused bites could incorporate dried mango, sesame seeds, and a hint of matcha for an exotic twist. Each cultural interpretation reflects the regional ingredients, flavors, and culinary traditions that inspire these bites, showcasing the adaptability of this snack to different palates and preferences.

The digital age has brought about a cultural shift in how individuals approach fitness and nutrition, with social media platforms becoming hubs for sharing recipes, fitness journeys, and wellness tips. The hashtag #EnergyBites or #FuelYourWorkout is a virtual community where enthusiasts share their experiences with nutritious fruit bites, exchange recipe ideas, and showcase their creative variations. The online presence of these bite-sized delights has contributed to their popularity, creating a community of like-minded individuals who appreciate the balance of flavor, convenience, and nutritional benefits offered by these treats.

In conclusion, crafting nutritious fruit bites for training

represents a fusion of culinary creativity, nutritional wisdom, and functional convenience. From carefully selecting ingredients to the artful combination of flavors and textures, these bites encapsulate the essence of a well-rounded and energy-sustaining snack. Whether enjoyed as a pre-workout boost, a mid-session refuel, or a post-training recovery option, nutritious fruit bites are a testament to the enduring appeal of snacks that nourish the body, delight the palate, and support the pursuit of peak physical performance.

# CHAPTER VIII

# Special Occasion Recipes

## Birthday Cake Bonanza

Birthdays, the annual milestones that mark the passage of time, are celebrated with joy, laughter, and a time-honored tradition—the cutting of the birthday cake. With its symbolic candles, sugary delights, and creative designs, the birthday cake takes center stage in the festivities, becoming a focal point that embodies the essence of celebration and indulgence. This section embarks on a delightful exploration into the world of birthday cakes, unraveling the history, cultural significance, and sheer pleasure derived from the Birthday Cake Bonanza—a celebration of the artistry, flavors, and communal joy surrounding the iconic birthday dessert.

The tradition of celebrating birthdays with cakes can be traced back to ancient civilizations, where sweetened bread or cakes were presented to deities and celebrated individuals. However, the modern concept of the birthday cake as we know it today began to take shape in the 19th century. The Industrial Revolution brought about advancements in baking ingredients and techniques, making cakes more accessible to a broader audience. The Victorian era popularized elaborately decorated cakes, often adorned with intricate designs and symbolic embellishments. The advent of commercially available baking powder in the mid-19th century simplified the cake-making process, contributing to the widespread adoption of cakes as the centerpiece of birthday celebrations.

The birthday cake's cultural significance extends beyond its historical roots, becoming a universal symbol of joy, togetherness, and the expression of love. The act of presenting a birthday cake, often adorned with candles representing the celebrant's age, is a gesture that transcends cultural boundaries. The ritual of making a wish and blowing out the candles has become a cherished tradition, adding an element of magic and anticipation to the birthday celebration. Sharing a slice of cake with friends and family reinforces connection and camaraderie, creating lasting memories around the shared enjoyment of a sweet treat.

The evolution of birthday cakes has given rise to many styles, flavors, and artistic designs that cater to diverse tastes and preferences. Classic flavors such as vanilla and chocolate remain perennial favorites, offering a timeless appeal that resonates with a broad audience. However, the world of birthday cakes has expanded to include an array of exotic flavors, from red velvet and salted caramel to matcha and passion fruit. Incorporating diverse ingredients, fillings, and frostings adds a layer of sophistication and creativity, turning the birthday cake into a canvas for culinary artistry.

The art of cake decoration has witnessed a renaissance, fueled by the rise of cake artists, pastry chefs, and home bakers who transform cakes into stunning works of edible art. Fondant, a pliable icing for intricate designs and smooth finishes, has become famous for creating visually striking cakes. With its luscious texture and versatility, buttercream remains a beloved option for both professional and homemade cakes. The use of edible colors, food-safe paints, and edible prints allows for the customization of cakes to match themes, interests, or hobbies, transforming the birthday cake into a personalized expression of the celebrant's personality.

The Birthday Cake Bonanza is not limited to traditional tiered or sheet cakes; it encompasses various cake variations that cater to different preferences and occasions. Cupcakes, with their portions and charming designs, have become famous for birthday celebrations, offering a convenient and visually appealing alternative to traditional cakes. Bundt cakes, with their distinctive ring shape, provide a unique and elegant twist on the classic birthday cake. The emergence of "smash cakes" for first birthdays, where a small cake is prepared for the birthday child to enjoy freely and create a delightful mess, adds a touch of whimsy to the celebration.

The concept of thematic cakes has gained prominence, with designs inspired by popular culture, hobbies, or favorite characters. The possibilities are endless, from cakes shaped like superheroes and princesses to replicas of beloved landmarks or hobbies. The Birthday Cake Bonanza invites creativity, allowing bakers to explore unconventional shapes, structures, and designs that add an element of surprise and excitement to the celebratory moment.

In the contemporary era, the Birthday Cake Bonanza has been further amplified by the influence of social media, where platforms like Instagram and Pinterest showcase an abundance of visually stunning and innovative cake designs. Hashtags like #BirthdayCakeGoals and #CakeInspiration are virtual galleries where enthusiasts share their cake creations, exchange ideas, and draw inspiration from a global community of bakers and cake artists. The online presence of the Birthday Cake Bonanza has contributed to the democratization of cake decorating, empowering individuals to explore their creativity and share their cake masterpieces with a global audience.

Baking and presenting a birthday cake has become an expression of love and care, transcending cultural and linguistic barriers. In some cultures, the choice of ingredients and flavors carries symbolic significance. In Western traditions, the birthday cake often features candles equal to the celebrant's age, with the blowing out of the candles symbolizing the making of a wish. In Chinese culture, the birthday cake may be infused with ingredients with positive connotations, such as red bean paste, for good luck. In Indian traditions, certain types of sweets, like mithai, are preferred for birthday celebrations, reflecting regional culinary preferences.

The Birthday Cake Bonanza is not confined to private celebrations; it has permeated the public sphere, influencing trends in the hospitality and baking industries. Bakeries and cake shops offer an array of pre-designed birthday cakes that cater to different tastes and themes, providing a convenient option for those seeking a professionally crafted cake. The popularity of reality TV shows centered around cake decorating and baking competitions has further fueled public interest in elaborate and artistic cake designs. Celebrity chefs and influencers, with their social media presence, contribute to the fascination with extravagant and visually stunning cakes, inspiring amateur and professional bakers to push the boundaries of creativity.

The joy derived from the Birthday Cake Bonanza extends beyond the visual appeal and artistic expression to the sensory pleasure experienced when indulging in a slice of cake. The first cut into a birthday cake, revealing the layers, colors, and textures, becomes a moment of anticipation and delight. It is savoring each bite, whether the moist crumb of a chocolate cake or the lightness of a sponge cake and engages the taste buds in a sensory journey that culminates in a symphony of flavors. The frosting, rich and buttery or light and whipped, adds a decadent touch that elevates the cake-eating experience.

Regarding dietary considerations, the Birthday Cake Bonanza accommodates various preferences and restrictions. The rise of health-conscious and dietary-specific choices has given birth to cakes that cater to gluten-free, vegan, or low-sugar diets. Alternative flour, plant-based ingredients, and natural sweeteners offer options for those with specific dietary needs, ensuring everyone can enjoy the joy of birthday cake without compromising their nutritional goals or restrictions.

In conclusion, the Birthday Cake Bonanza celebrates joy, creativity, and the shared delight derived from the iconic birthday dessert. From its historical roots to the modern era of elaborate cake designs, the birthday cake symbolizes celebration, love, and the simple pleasure of enjoying a sweet treat with loved ones. Whether adorned with intricate designs or kept simple and classic, the birthday cake is a timeless tradition that transcends cultural and generational boundaries—a testament to the enduring joy and significance of marking life's milestones with a slice of cake.

## Holiday Feasts for Your Furry Friend

As the holiday season approaches, the joy of festive feasting extends beyond human gatherings to include our beloved furry companions. Pet owners worldwide embrace the tradition of treating their pets to special meals, ensuring that the joy and warmth of the holidays are shared with every family member. This section embarks on a delightful exploration of holiday feasts explicitly designed for our four-legged friends—a celebration of culinary creativity, nutritional considerations, and the shared joy from treating our pets to a festive dining experience.

Preparing holiday feasts for pets is rooted in the deep bond between humans and their animal companions. Often considered integral family members, pets bring companionship, loyalty, and unconditional love. As the holiday season unfolds, the desire to include them in the festivities naturally extends to their culinary experiences. The tradition of crafting special meals for pets during the holidays reflects a sentiment of care, gratitude, and a shared sense of celebration that transcends species boundaries.

The holiday feasts for furry friends are characterized by a thoughtful selection of ingredients that cater to the nutritional needs of pets while incorporating flavors that appeal to their discerning palates. High-quality proteins, such as lean meats or fish, serve as the foundation, providing essential amino acids that support muscle health and overall well-being. Whole grains, vegetables, and fruits contribute fiber, vitamins, and minerals, offering a well-rounded nutritional profile. Using pet-safe herbs, such as parsley or mint, enhances flavor and introduces potential digestive benefits.

The crafting process involves a delicate balance of culinary creativity and adherence to pet-specific dietary guidelines. Recipes for holiday feasts often prioritize simplicity and avoid including ingredients harmful to pets, such as onions, garlic, or excessive amounts of certain spices. The choice of cooking methods, whether baking, boiling, or steaming, aims to preserve the nutritional integrity of the ingredients while ensuring their digestibility for our furry companions. The presentation of the feast may involve shaping or arranging pet-friendly ingredients into visually appealing forms, adding an element of fun and festivity to the dining experience.

The nutritional considerations for holiday feasts extend beyond flavor to encompass pets' overall well-being. Including vegetables and fruits provides a source of vitamins, antioxidants, and fiber, supporting digestive health and immune function. Omega-3 fatty acids from fish contribute to a healthy coat and skin, while lean proteins aid in muscle development and maintenance. The absence of excessive fats and salts aligns to promote balanced and wholesome nutrition for pets, ensuring that the festive feasts contribute positively to their overall health.

The joy derived from sharing holiday feasts with furry friends is not limited to preparing and presenting the meals; it extends to the shared experience of witnessing their enjoyment. The anticipation in their eyes, the wagging tails, and the eagerness they approach their festive bowls create moments of pure delight for pet owners. The communal act of celebrating the holidays with pets through shared meals fosters a sense of connection and mutual enjoyment, reinforcing the bond between humans and their animal companions.

The variety of holiday feasts for pets is as diverse as the culinary creativity of pet owners. The options are vast, from homemade treats and cookies shaped like holiday symbols to elaborate meals featuring a mix of proteins, grains, and vegetables. Some pet owners may prepare festive meals as a standalone dining experience. In contrast, others incorporate pet-friendly elements into their holiday meals, allowing pets to partake in the shared joy of the season. The flexibility in recipes and presentation ensures that pet holiday feasts can be tailored to suit individual preferences, dietary needs, and the specific tastes of each furry friend.

The holiday feasts for pets find resonance in the broader cultural shift toward viewing pets not just as animals but as cherished family members. The market for pet-specific treats, meals, and accessories has experienced significant growth, reflecting pet owners' increased awareness and willingness to invest in their furry companions' well-being and happiness. Pet-centric holidays, such as "Barksgiving" and "Meow Year's Eve," have emerged as occasions for pampering pets with special treats and meals, further solidifying the trend of including pets in holiday celebrations.

The digital age has played a significant role in amplifying the celebration of pet holiday feasts, with social media platforms serving as virtual hubs for pet owners to share their culinary creations and experiences. Hashtags such as #PetFeast and #FurryHolidayFeast become online communities where pet owners exchange ideas, recipes, and images of their furry friends enjoying special meals. The online presence of festive pet feasts contributes to a shared celebration, creating a global community that appreciates the joy of treating pets to culinary delights during the holidays.

Regarding dietary inclusivity, pet holiday feasts accommodate various dietary preferences and restrictions. The availability of pet-friendly recipes for those with allergies, sensitivities, or specific nutritional needs ensures that all pets can partake in the holiday festivities. Grain-free options, protein-specific recipes, and treats tailored to individual preferences allow pet owners to cater to their furry friends' unique nutritional requirements and taste preferences, creating a personalized and inclusive dining experience.

Preparing holiday feasts for pets goes beyond nutrition; it becomes a gesture of love, gratitude, and reciprocity. Pets, with their unconditional affection and companionship, enrich the lives of their human counterparts. The holidays, emphasizing gratitude and giving, allow pet owners to express their appreciation for the joy and comfort pets bring. Crafting festive meals becomes a tangible expression of this gratitude, creating a shared celebration and indulgence.

In conclusion, holiday feasts for furry friends represent a heartwarming celebration of the bond between humans and their animal companions. From the careful selection of ingredients to the thoughtful preparation and presentation of festive meals, treating pets to unique culinary delights becomes a shared experience that enhances the joy of the holiday season. Whether it's a simple treat, a festive meal, or a creative arrangement of pet-friendly ingredients, the holiday feast for pets embodies the spirit of love, connection, and joy derived from celebrating the holidays with every family member—furry or not.

## Celebrating Milestones with Tail-Wagging Treats

In the journey of companionship with our four-legged friends, every milestone they achieve is a cause for celebration. Whether it's a birthday, an adoption anniversary, or a training triumph, pet owners commemorate these special moments with gestures of love and appreciation. One delightful tradition that has gained popularity is celebrating milestones with tail-wagging treats—culinary indulgences explicitly designed to mark the achievements and milestones of our beloved pets. This section embarks on a heartwarming exploration of the significance, creativity, and shared joy of celebrating milestones through the artful crafting of special treats for our furry companions.

Celebrating milestones with treats is rooted in the deep connection between humans and their pets. Often considered family members, pets weave their way into our hearts with their loyalty, affection, and unique personalities. Our pets' achievements and milestones become sources of pride and joy as we travel through life together. In response, pet owners seek to express their love and appreciation through gestures beyond the routine, marking these milestones as occasions for special recognition and celebration.

Tail-wagging treats designed for milestone celebrations are characterized by a thoughtful selection of ingredients that cater to pets' specific tastes and nutritional needs. High-quality proteins, such as lean meats or fish, form the foundation, contributing essential amino acids for muscle health and overall well-being. Whole grains, vegetables, and fruits provide fiber, vitamins, and minerals, creating a well-rounded nutritional profile. Using pet-safe herbs and spices, such as parsley or cinnamon, adds flavor and offers potential digestive or health benefits.

The crafting process of milestone treats involves a blend of culinary creativity and understanding pet-specific dietary guidelines. Pet owners often prioritize safe and beneficial ingredients for their furry friends, avoiding potential hazards such as chocolate, onions, or excessive amounts of salt. The recipes may vary based on the milestone being celebrated—whether it's a "Gotcha Day" adoption anniversary or a "Good Dog" achievement in training. The treats may be shaped, decorated, or arranged in a way that adds a festive touch to the celebration, creating an experience that is both flavorful and visually delightful for the pets.

The joy derived from celebrating milestones with tail-wagging treats extends beyond preparation to the shared experience of witnessing the pets' enjoyment. The enthusiasm in their eyes, the eager anticipation as they catch a whiff of the treats, and the sheer delight as they savor each bite create precious moments for pet owners. The shared celebration becomes a bonding experience, reinforcing the connection between humans and their pets through the simple yet profound language of treats and affection.

The variety of milestone treats is as diverse as the milestones themselves, showcasing the culinary creativity of pet owners. The options are vast, from homemade biscuits and cupcakes to frozen treats and chewy bites. Some pet owners may celebrate birthdays with personalized cakes or cupcakes, while others might commemorate training successes with savory treats that double as rewards. The flexibility in recipes and presentation ensures that milestone treats can be tailored to suit individual preferences, dietary needs, and the specific tastes of each furry friend.

The tradition of celebrating milestones with treats has found resonance in the broader cultural shift toward viewing pets as animals and as cherished family members. Pet-centric occasions, such as "Bark Mitzvahs" or "Pawties," have emerged, reflecting the desire of pet owners to go beyond routine care and celebrate the unique milestones in their pets' lives. The market for specialty pet treats and bakery items has experienced significant growth, offering pet owners a wide array of options to choose from or inspiring them to embark on culinary adventures for their furry friends.

The digital age has played a significant role in amplifying the celebration of milestones with tail-wagging treats, with social media platforms serving as virtual showcases for pet owners to share their creations and experiences. Hashtags like #PawtyTime and #PetMilestone celebrate the joy of marking special moments with treats, creating online communities where pet owners can exchange ideas, recipes, and images of their pets enjoying special treats. The online presence of these celebrations contributes to a sense of shared joy and inspiration, creating a global community that appreciates the art of celebrating milestones with our four-legged companions.

In dietary inclusivity, milestone treats accommodate a spectrum of preferences and restrictions. The availability of pet-friendly recipes for those with allergies, sensitivities, or specific nutritional needs ensures that all pets can partake in the joy of milestone celebrations.

Grain-free options, protein-specific recipes, and treats tailored to individual preferences allow pet owners to cater to their furry friends' unique nutritional requirements and taste preferences, creating a personalized and inclusive experience.

Beyond the culinary aspects, celebrating milestones with treats becomes a gesture of acknowledgment and positive reinforcement for pets. Dogs, in particular, respond positively to praise, treats, and attention, making celebrating their achievements a form of communication that strengthens the human-animal bond. Whether it's a well-behaved pup graduating from obedience school or a senior pet reaching a health milestone, the treats serve as tangible expressions of love and appreciation, creating positive associations with the milestones.

In conclusion, celebrating milestones with tail-wagging treats is a heartwarming tradition that exemplifies the joy, creativity, and shared moments of happiness between pet owners and their beloved companions. From carefully selecting ingredients to the thoughtful crafting of treats, celebrating milestones becomes a sensory experience that engages humans and pets in a shared celebration. Whether it's a simple homemade biscuit or an elaborate cupcake, the treats serve as edible tokens of love and recognition, making every milestone a positively sweet occasion in the journey of companionship.

# CHAPTER IX

# Dealing with Dietary Restrictions

## Allergies and Sensitivities in Dogs

Canine health is a multifaceted journey, marked by the pursuit of optimal well-being and the fulfillment of specific nutritional needs. In this intricate tapestry of care, allergies and sensitivities stand out as significant considerations, requiring a nuanced understanding from dog owners and caregivers. This section delves into the realm of allergies and sensitivities in dogs—a complex interplay of genetics, environment, and dietary factors that necessitates attention, diagnosis, and thoughtful management for the holistic health of our furry companions.

Allergies in dogs are manifestations of the immune system's response to substances that are typically harmless but perceived as threats. These substances, known as allergens, can trigger an immune reaction leading to a range of symptoms. The most common types of allergies in dogs include food allergies, environmental allergies (such as pollen or dust mites), and contact allergies (resulting from direct skin contact with certain substances). Sensitivities, on the other hand, often refer to adverse reactions that may not involve the immune system but still cause discomfort or digestive issues.

Food allergies and sensitivities are prevalent concerns in the realm of canine health. Dogs, like humans, can develop sensitivities or allergies to specific ingredients in their diet. Common allergens include proteins such as beef, chicken, and dairy, as well as grains like wheat and corn. Identifying the culprit in a dog's diet requires a methodical approach, often involving elimination diets or specialized testing. The symptoms of food allergies or sensitivities in dogs can manifest in various ways, including gastrointestinal issues like diarrhea or vomiting, dermatological problems like itching or skin inflammation, and even behavioral changes.

Environmental allergies, often referred to as atopic dermatitis, result from a dog's hypersensitivity to airborne particles like pollen, mold spores, or dust mites. These allergies typically manifest as skin-related issues, with dogs exhibiting symptoms such as itching, redness, and recurrent ear infections. While environmental allergies are more challenging to manage since complete avoidance is nearly impossible, various treatment options, including antihistamines and immunotherapy, can help alleviate symptoms and improve a dog's quality of life.

Contact allergies involve adverse reactions to substances that come into direct contact with a dog's skin. Common culprits include certain cleaning products, fabrics, or grooming products. Identifying and eliminating the source of the contact allergy is essential for preventing recurring skin issues or discomfort. Additionally, veterinarians may recommend hypoallergenic grooming products or alternative materials to minimize the risk of contact allergies.

Genetics play a pivotal role in a dog's predisposition to allergies, with certain breeds being more susceptible than others. Breeds like the Labrador Retriever, Golden Retriever, and German Shepherd are known to have a higher likelihood of developing allergies. However, allergies can affect any dog, regardless of breed or lineage. Understanding a dog's genetic predisposition can assist veterinarians in anticipating potential health issues and implementing preventive measures.

Diagnosing allergies and sensitivities in dogs requires a collaborative effort between pet owners and veterinary professionals. A thorough medical history, including dietary habits, environmental exposures, and previous health concerns, serves as a foundational element in the diagnostic process. Veterinarians may recommend various diagnostic tools, including blood tests, skin tests, and elimination diets, to pinpoint the specific allergens triggering a dog's reactions. The process may involve trial and error, as identifying the source of allergies can be a nuanced and time-consuming endeavor.

The management of allergies and sensitivities in dogs often involves a multifaceted approach that addresses both the symptoms and the underlying causes. Dietary modifications, such as transitioning to hypoallergenic or limited-ingredient diets, are common strategies for managing food allergies. These specialized diets aim to minimize exposure to potential allergens and provide a balanced nutritional profile to support the dog's overall health. In severe cases, prescription diets formulated for dogs with food sensitivities may be recommended.

Environmental allergies may require a combination of lifestyle adjustments and medical interventions. Regular grooming practices, including bathing and brushing, can help remove potential allergens from a dog's coat. Additionally, the use of air purifiers, allergen-resistant bedding, and minimizing outdoor exposure during peak allergen seasons can contribute to symptom management. Medications such as antihistamines or corticosteroids may be prescribed to alleviate itching and inflammation.

Contact allergies often necessitate identifying and eliminating the source of irritation. Using hypoallergenic grooming products, selecting pet-friendly cleaning supplies, and avoiding materials known to trigger reactions can significantly reduce the risk of contact allergies. In cases where a dog has developed a skin infection due to excessive itching or scratching, veterinarians may prescribe antibiotics or topical treatments to address secondary infections.

Immunotherapy, commonly known as allergy shots, is a long-term treatment option for dogs with environmental allergies. This approach involves exposing the dog to gradually increasing amounts of the identified allergens, desensitizing the immune system over time. While not a cure, immunotherapy can significantly reduce the severity of symptoms and improve a dog's quality of life. Regular veterinary check-ups and ongoing communication between pet owners and veterinarians are crucial for assessing the effectiveness of the chosen management strategies and adjusting them as needed.

The role of nutrition in managing allergies and sensitivities in dogs cannot be overstated. Specialized diets formulated for dogs with food allergies or sensitivities often feature novel protein sources, such as venison or duck, and limited ingredient lists to minimize the risk of triggering allergic reactions. Grain-free options or diets containing easily digestible carbohydrates may be recommended, depending on the dog's specific dietary needs. Nutrition not only plays a key role in managing allergies but also contributes to overall immune system health and resilience.

Holistic approaches to managing allergies and sensitivities in dogs encompass lifestyle factors that contribute to a dog's overall well-being. Regular exercise, mental stimulation, and a stress-free environment can positively impact a dog's immune function and help mitigate the effects of allergies. Maintaining optimal weight and overall health through a balanced diet and regular veterinary check-ups is crucial for supporting a dog's ability to cope with allergies and sensitivities.

The prevalence of allergies and sensitivities in dogs has prompted the pet industry to evolve, offering a plethora of specialized products and services to cater to the unique needs of allergic or sensitive individuals. From hypoallergenic grooming products and shampoos to allergen-resistant bedding and air purifiers, pet owners have access to a range of tools designed to create environments that minimize potential triggers. Additionally, the market for novel protein sources and limited-ingredient diets has expanded, providing pet owners with diverse options to tailor their dogs' diets to specific nutritional requirements.

In conclusion, allergies and sensitivities in dogs represent a multifaceted aspect of canine health that requires a comprehensive understanding, proactive management, and ongoing collaboration between pet owners and veterinary professionals. The journey of navigating allergies involves careful observation, diagnostic precision, and the implementation of tailored strategies to address the specific needs of each dog. With a commitment to understanding the nuances of canine health, pet owners can ensure that their furry companions lead fulfilling lives free from the discomfort and challenges posed by allergies and sensitivities.

## Tailoring Recipes for Specific Health Conditions

The bond between humans and their canine companions is often woven through shared experiences, and one of the most intimate connections is forged in the act of nourishing. As responsible pet owners, understanding the unique dietary needs of our dogs becomes paramount, especially when faced with specific health conditions that necessitate tailored nutritional approaches. This section embarks on a journey into the art of tailoring recipes for specific health conditions in dogs—a meticulous and thoughtful process that combines culinary creativity with a commitment to canine well-being.

Dogs, like humans, may encounter a myriad of health conditions throughout their lives, ranging from allergies and gastrointestinal issues to chronic diseases like diabetes or kidney disease. In response to these challenges, pet owners and caregivers find themselves in the position of crafting diets that not only meet the basic nutritional requirements of their furry friends but also address specific health concerns. The art of tailoring recipes for specific health conditions requires an understanding of canine physiology, dietary guidelines from veterinary professionals, and a willingness to explore alternative ingredients and cooking techniques.

When faced with health conditions such as food allergies or sensitivities, pet owners often embark on the journey of creating recipes that eliminate potential allergens and provide a balanced nutritional profile. The focus may shift to novel protein sources, such as venison or rabbit, and easily digestible carbohydrates like sweet potatoes or quinoa. These recipes aim to minimize the risk of triggering allergic reactions while ensuring that the dog receives essential nutrients for overall health. The culinary precision involved in selecting ingredients becomes a crucial aspect of managing health conditions and improving the dog's quality of life.

For dogs diagnosed with chronic conditions like diabetes, dietary considerations extend beyond managing specific symptoms to regulating blood sugar levels and maintaining overall health. Recipes tailored for diabetic dogs often prioritize complex carbohydrates with a low glycemic index, such as lentils or barley, to promote stable blood sugar levels. Proteins from sources like lean meats and fish contribute to muscle health, while fiber-rich vegetables aid in digestion and weight management. The meticulous balancing of macronutrients becomes an integral part of crafting recipes that support dogs with diabetes, aligning with both nutritional and medical requirements.

Canine kidney disease presents another challenge that demands a nuanced approach to dietary management. Recipes tailored for dogs with kidney issues focus on reducing phosphorus levels, as excessive phosphorus can exacerbate kidney damage. Additionally, the inclusion of high-quality proteins, controlled sodium levels, and omega-3 fatty acids becomes crucial in supporting kidney function and managing symptoms. Crafting recipes for dogs with kidney disease involves not only meeting nutritional goals but also ensuring palatability to encourage adequate food intake—a delicate balance that requires both culinary skill and a deep understanding of the dog's health condition.

The prevalence of gastrointestinal issues in dogs underscores the importance of tailoring recipes to promote digestive health. Dogs with sensitive stomachs or chronic gastrointestinal conditions may benefit from recipes that incorporate easily digestible proteins, such as chicken or turkey, and bland carbohydrates like rice or pumpkin. The inclusion of probiotics or prebiotics, either through specific ingredients or supplements, can support a healthy gut microbiome and aid in digestion. Tailoring recipes for dogs with gastrointestinal concerns requires a focus on both nutrient density and digestive ease, striking a balance that promotes overall wellness.

In the realm of aging and senior dogs, the focus shifts towards recipes that support joint health, cognitive function, and overall vitality. Ingredients rich in antioxidants, such as blueberries or spinach, contribute to combating oxidative stress associated with aging. Omega-3 fatty acids from fish or flaxseed oil support joint mobility and cardiovascular health. Protein sources with high bioavailability, like eggs or lean meats, become essential for maintaining muscle mass and supporting aging dogs' unique nutritional needs. Crafting recipes for senior dogs becomes a celebration of their life journey, recognizing the changing dynamics of health and adjusting nutrition accordingly.

The art of tailoring recipes for specific health conditions in dogs is not confined to physical health alone; it also extends to the realm of mental and emotional well-being. Dogs experiencing stress, anxiety, or behavioral issues may benefit from recipes that include ingredients known for their calming properties. For example, incorporating ingredients like chamomile, ginger, or turmeric into recipes can have a soothing effect on dogs' nervous systems. The consideration of holistic well-being in recipe tailoring underscores the interconnectedness of physical and mental health, emphasizing the role of nutrition in supporting dogs' overall quality of life.

The process of tailoring recipes for specific health conditions necessitates collaboration between pet owners and veterinary professionals. A thorough understanding of the dog's health history, diagnostic information, and nutritional requirements forms the foundation for crafting recipes that align with both medical guidelines and the dog's individual needs. Veterinary consultations provide crucial insights into dietary modifications, recommended nutrient profiles, and potential supplementations that can enhance the efficacy of tailored recipes. This collaborative approach ensures that the recipes not only address specific health conditions but also contribute positively to the dog's overall health and vitality.

The digital age has played a pivotal role in amplifying the discourse around tailoring recipes for specific health conditions in dogs. Online communities, forums, and social media platforms serve as virtual hubs where pet owners share their experiences, exchange recipes, and seek advice from others facing similar challenges. Hashtags such as #CanineWellness and #HealthyRecipesForDogs have become channels for disseminating knowledge, fostering a sense of community, and inspiring pet owners to explore new culinary horizons in support of their dogs' health.

As the awareness of canine nutrition and health continues to grow, the pet industry has responded by offering a myriad of specialized products and services. From commercially available prescription diets formulated for specific health conditions to a wide array of supplements targeting joint health, skin issues, or digestive support, pet owners have access to resources that complement their efforts in tailoring recipes. The market's evolution reflects a collective commitment to enhancing canine well-being through the integration of culinary precision, nutritional expertise, and a genuine concern for the health and happiness of our four-legged companions.

In conclusion, the art of tailoring recipes for specific health conditions in dogs is a testament to the evolving understanding of canine nutrition and health. It requires a delicate balance of culinary creativity, nutritional science, and a deep connection with the unique needs of individual dogs. As pet owners embrace the responsibility of nourishing their canine companions, the process of crafting tailored recipes becomes an expression of love, care, and a commitment to supporting dogs in their journey toward optimal well-being.

## Consulting with a Veterinarian for Special Diets

The relationship between dogs and their human companions is one of profound connection, built on shared experiences, trust, and care. Nowhere is this bond more evident than in the realm of nutrition, where pet owners play a pivotal role in shaping the health and well- being of their canine friends. In instances where special diets are deemed necessary—whether due to medical conditions, dietary restrictions, or unique nutritional needs—seeking the guidance of a veterinarian becomes not just a responsible choice but a crucial step toward ensuring the optimal health and happiness of our four- legged companions.

The decision to embark on a special diet journey for a dog may arise from various circumstances, each requiring a tailored approach to nutrition. Medical conditions such as allergies, diabetes, kidney disease, or gastrointestinal issues may necessitate specific dietary modifications to manage symptoms and promote overall health. Similarly, dogs with unique nutritional requirements, such as seniors, puppies, or those with breed-specific sensitivities, benefit from diets carefully crafted to meet their individual needs. In any case, the journey toward a special diet begins with a fundamental understanding of the importance of consulting with a veterinarian—a professional equipped with the knowledge and expertise to guide pet owners through the intricacies of canine nutrition.

Veterinarians serve as invaluable partners in the process of designing and implementing special diets for dogs. Their role extends beyond diagnosing medical conditions or providing routine care; it encompasses a comprehensive understanding of each dog's unique health profile, dietary requirements, and lifestyle. When faced with the prospect of a special diet, the first step for pet owners is to engage in open and transparent communication with their veterinarian. This initial consultation serves as a crucial foundation for the development of a tailored dietary plan that aligns with the dog's specific needs and health goals.

During the consultation, veterinarians conduct a thorough assessment of the dog's health, taking into account factors such as age, breed, weight, activity level, and any existing medical conditions. This holistic approach ensures that the dietary recommendations not only address immediate concerns but also contribute to the dog's long-term well-being. The exchange of information between pet owners and veterinarians becomes a collaborative effort, with both parties sharing insights, concerns, and observations that contribute to a comprehensive understanding of the dog's health status.

For dogs with medical conditions, such as allergies or diabetes, the consultation with a veterinarian is instrumental in identifying dietary triggers and establishing nutritional guidelines that mitigate symptoms. In cases of food allergies, veterinarians may recommend elimination diets or allergy testing to pinpoint specific allergens. Diabetic dogs benefit from diets that regulate blood sugar levels, incorporating complex carbohydrates, high-quality proteins, and controlled portions. The veterinarian's expertise ensures that the special diet not only aligns with the dog's medical needs but also provides a foundation for holistic health.

Canine kidney disease represents another area where consulting with a veterinarian for a special diet is essential. Veterinarians guide pet owners in crafting diets that manage phosphorus levels, reduce sodium intake, and provide high-quality proteins with optimal bioavailability. The tailored approach to nutrition aims to support kidney function, alleviate symptoms, and enhance the dog's quality of life. The nuanced understanding of the dog's specific health condition allows veterinarians to recommend dietary modifications that contribute to long-term renal health.

Puppies and senior dogs, with their distinct nutritional requirements, also benefit significantly from the expertise of veterinarians in the realm of special diets. Puppies undergo rapid growth and development, necessitating diets rich in essential nutrients, including proteins, vitamins, and minerals. Veterinarians guide pet owners in selecting appropriate puppy diets that foster healthy growth without compromising their overall well-being. Similarly, senior dogs may experience changes in metabolism, joint health, and cognitive function, requiring special diets that address these specific needs. Consulting with a veterinarian ensures that the dietary plan for puppies and seniors aligns with their unique life stages and promotes optimal health.

While medical conditions and life stages often prompt the need for special diets, some dogs may have breed-specific sensitivities or dietary preferences that warrant a customized approach. Certain breeds are known to be more susceptible to allergies or sensitivities, making it essential for veterinarians to consider these factors when formulating dietary recommendations. Additionally, some dogs may simply have preferences or aversions to certain ingredients, textures, or flavors. The veterinarian's role extends beyond addressing medical concerns to creating a dietary plan that is not only nutritionally sound but also palatable and enjoyable for the dog.

The expertise of veterinarians in tailoring special diets is complemented by their knowledge of the dynamic landscape of pet nutrition. The pet food industry continually evolves, introducing new formulations, ingredients, and dietary trends. Veterinarians stay abreast of these developments, enabling them to provide informed and up-to-date recommendations to pet owners. This dynamic approach ensures that special diets for dogs are not only based on established principles of nutrition but also integrate the latest advancements in the field.

Beyond the prescription of commercial therapeutic diets, veterinarians play a crucial role in guiding pet owners through the process of preparing homemade or home-cooked diets tailored to specific health conditions. The meticulous crafting of recipes involves selecting ingredients that align with the dog's nutritional requirements and dietary restrictions. Veterinarians offer guidance on ingredient choices, portion control, and cooking methods, ensuring that homemade diets are nutritionally complete and safe for long-term use. This personalized approach acknowledges the diversity of canine palates and allows pet owners to actively participate in their dogs' nutritional care.

The collaborative relationship between pet owners and veterinarians extends beyond the initial consultation to include ongoing communication and follow-up appointments. Regular check-ups allow veterinarians to monitor the dog's response to the special diet, make necessary adjustments, and address any emerging health concerns. This continuous dialogue fosters a sense of partnership and shared responsibility for the dog's health journey. Pet owners are encouraged to share observations, ask questions, and actively engage in discussions about their dogs' nutritional well-being.

The digital age has ushered in new avenues for pet owners to access information and resources related to special diets for dogs. Online platforms, forums, and social media communities serve as virtual spaces where pet owners can share experiences, seek advice, and exchange recipes. While these digital resources can offer valuable insights and a sense of community, they do not replace the expertise and personalized care provided by a veterinarian. The internet landscape is vast and varied, making it essential for pet owners to critically evaluate the reliability of information and consult with their veterinarians for context-specific guidance.

The significance of consulting with a veterinarian for

special diets transcends the realms of medical care and nutrition—it embodies a commitment to the holistic well-being of our canine companions. The special diet journey, guided by veterinary expertise, becomes a testament to the dedication of pet owners in ensuring that their dogs receive the care and nourishment they deserve. The veterinarian's role extends beyond that of a healthcare provider; it encompasses that of a trusted advisor, collaborator, and advocate for the furry family members under their care.

In conclusion, the journey of tailoring special diets for dogs underscores the importance of collaborative care between pet owners and veterinarians. From the initial consultation to ongoing communication and follow-up appointments, the partnership between pet owners and veterinarians is a cornerstone of canine health and well-being. In embracing the guidance of veterinarians, pet owners embark on a journey that combines scientific knowledge, culinary precision, and a shared commitment to nurturing the health and happiness of their beloved dogs.

# CONCLUSION

In the delightful journey through "Tail-Wagging Treats: A DIY Dog Food Feast - Simple Recipes for a Healthy and Happy Pup," readers have been invited into a world where the art of crafting canine culinary delights becomes an expression of love, care, and shared joy. This e-book, a treasure trove of simple recipes for homemade dog treats, encapsulates the essence of fostering a healthy and happy bond with our four-legged companions.

As we've explored the pages of this e-book, the significance of tailoring treats to meet the specific needs and tastes of our dogs has emerged as a central theme. From protein-packed breakfast bowls to frozen yogurt pops for summer, each recipe is a testament to the dedication of pet owners in providing not just nourishment but moments of sheer delight for their furry friends. The careful selection of ingredients, the thoughtful consideration of dietary requirements, and the creative presentation of treats exemplify the holistic approach to canine well-being.

The e-book goes beyond being a mere collection of recipes; it is a celebration of the unique relationship between humans and dogs. Whether marking milestones with homemade biscuits or indulging in a gourmet meatloaf, the act of preparing and sharing treats becomes a language of love that transcends the boundaries of species. It's a recognition that our dogs are not just pets but cherished family members, deserving of the best we can offer in terms of nutrition, care, and affection.

In the world of DIY dog food feasts, this e-book stands as a guide, encouraging pet owners to explore their culinary creativity, embrace nutritional mindfulness, and savor the joy that comes with seeing a tail-wagging, tongue-lolling approval from their furry companions. With simplicity as its ethos and the well-being of our pups at its heart, "Tail-Wagging Treats" is more than a cookbook; it is an invitation to embark on a culinary adventure that enriches the lives of both pet owners and their canine friends. As we conclude this delightful journey, let it be a reminder that the path to a happy and healthy pup is paved with love, homemade treats, and shared moments of sheer canine delight.

*Thank you for buying and reading/listening to our book. If you found this book useful/helpful please take a few minutes and leave a review on the platform where you purchased our book. Your feedback matters greatly to us.*

www.ingramcontent.com/pod-product-compliance
Lightning Source LLC
Chambersburg PA
CBHW052053150726
48002CB00002B/877